T0054650

BREAKING THE PROMISE OF *BROWN*

BREAKING
THE PROMISE
OF *BROWN*

The Resegregation of
America's Schools

Jᴜstice Stephen Breyer

Introduction by Thiru Vignarajah

BROOKINGS INSTITUTION PRESS
Washington, D.C.

Copyright © 2022
THE BROOKINGS INSTITUTION
1775 Massachusetts Avenue, N.W., Washington, D.C. 20036
www.brookings.edu

All rights reserved. No part of this publication may be reproduced or transmitted in any form or by any means without permission in writing from the Brookings Institution Press.

The Brookings Institution is a private nonprofit organization devoted to research, education, and publication on important issues of domestic and foreign policy. Its principal purpose is to bring the highest quality independent research and analysis to bear on current and emerging policy problems. Interpretations or conclusions in Brookings publications should be understood to be solely those of the authors.

This book reprints Justice Stephen Breyer's dissent in *Parents Involved in Community Schools v. Seattle School District No. 1*, 127 S. Ct. 2738 (2007), taken from the public record. Justice Breyer does not receive any compensation or remuneration for this book. The Brookings Institution has published Stephen Breyer's work since the 1970s: Stephen G. Breyer and Paul W. MacAvoy, *Energy Regulation by the Federal Power Commission*, 1974; Stephen Breyer, *Economic Reasoning and Judicial Review*, 2004.

Library of Congress Control Number: 2021970078

9 8 7 6 5 4 3 2 1

Typeset in Sabon

CONTENTS

INTRODUCTION
Thiru Vignarajah
1

JUSTICE BREYER'S DISSENT
IN THE RESEGREGATION CASES
39

APPENDIX A: RESEGREGATION TRENDS
102

APPENDIX B: SOURCES FOR
PARTS I-A AND I-B
106

NOTES TO JUSTICE BREYER'S DISSENT
IN THE RESEGREGATION CASES
110

INDEX
123

BREAKING THE PROMISE OF *BROWN*

INTRODUCTION
THIRU VIGNARAJAH

THE PROMISE OF *BROWN*

For *Brown v. Board of Education* held out a promise.
It was a promise embodied in three Amendments designed to make citizens of slaves. It was the promise of
true racial equality—not as a matter of fine words on
paper, but as a matter of everyday life in the Nation's
cities and schools.[1]

The worst kept secret in America is that our nation's schools
remain stubbornly segregated by race.

Over 8.4 million Black and Latino students—40 percent of
those students nationwide—attend public schools that are more
than 90 percent minority. Nearly a third of those students go to
schools that are less than 1 percent white. These are the same
malnourished schools that have been neglected for decades,
yielding low test scores, high suspension rates, and bleak career and college opportunities for three generations of minority
schoolchildren.

The consequences are everywhere. Maps of crime, unem-
ployment, and disease mirror racial disparities in schools. Righ-

1. *Parents Involved in Community Schools v. Seattle School District
No. 1*, 551 U.S. 701, 867 (2007) (Breyer, J., dissenting).

1

teous fury boiling over on American streets and the toxic state of race relations in parts of the country are fueled—perhaps even preordained—by the black-and-white checkerboard pattern of our schools. How can this be the modern legacy of the civil rights movement?

After all, long-standing inequities and racial tensions were meant to recede as one generation's prejudices surrendered to the tolerance of the next. Tolerance was to be cultivated on vibrant playgrounds full of children learning and laughing with companions of many races. That has not been the American story. Instead, hundreds of thousands of classrooms remain as segregated today as they were before *Brown v. Board of Education*.

The present conditions are not transient or novel or accidental. They have persisted for fifty years because we have let them. And the U.S. Supreme Court is not free from blame. The very institution that first proclaimed and then doggedly pursued the promise of *Brown* has, despite formidable dissents by some of history's great jurists, allowed its breach and retreat.

In 2007, local efforts to correct this dismal reality suffered a significant setback. In a jarring upheaval of settled law, the Supreme Court struck down two promising school board initiatives designed to combat the risk of resegregation and achieve more inclusive schools. The 5-4 decision in *Parents Involved in Community Schools v. Seattle School District No. 1* and its companion case out of Louisville, Kentucky—together, what I call the "Resegregation Cases"—marked the end of an era of efforts by school authorities to fulfill the promise of racially integrated education once imagined in *Brown*.[2]

The Resegregation Cases concerned high schools in Seat-

2. *Brown v. Board of Education*, 347 U.S. 483 (1954).

tle and elementary schools in Louisville that were undeniably polarized by race. Convinced that schoolchildren benefit from diverse classrooms, local authorities adopted school choice and school transfer policies, accompanied by race-conscious restrictions, to promote integration. A sharply divided Supreme Court ruled that these initiatives, no matter their good intentions, were forbidden by the Constitution.

In a searing landmark dissent, Justice Stephen Breyer warned this was "a decision the Court and the Nation will come to regret." Fifteen years later, the unabated resegregation of America's schools has confirmed Justice Breyer's fears, as many schools and school districts across the country are more racially segregated today than they have been since the late 1960s.

This volume contains Justice Breyer's dissent in its entirety. It is the longest opinion—majority or dissent—of his career. For this son of a school board lawyer, it is also his most inspired. *New York Times* legal reporter Linda Greenhouse said those in the courtroom on the day of the decision had never heard Justice Breyer "express himself with such emotion."[3] Justice John Paul Stevens wrote that Breyer's dissent was "eloquent and unanswerable."[4] Another justice called it "the finest thing any of us on the current Court has ever done."[5] One of Justice Thurgood Marshall's sons privately thanked Justice Breyer for his "wisdom, judgment, strength and courage"[6] and shared that the opinion brought him to tears.

3. Linda Greenhouse, "Justices Reject Diversity Plans in Two Districts" (*New York Times*, June 28, 2007).

4. *Parents Involved in Community Schools v. Seattle School District No. 1*, 551 U.S. 701, 798 (2007) (Stevens, J., dissenting).

5. Letter from Associate Justice of the Supreme Court, to Justice Stephen G. Breyer (June 26, 2007).

6. Letter from Thurgood Marshall Jr. to Justice Stephen G. Breyer (June 28, 2007).

June 28

Dear Justice Breyer,

I once shed a tear in a courtroom. I had just been sworn into the Supreme Court bar upon my father's motion during his last term. I happened to glance over and saw that my mother had snuck in my son Thurgood William (then 2½) to witness the occasion — the only time that the three of us would find ourselves in that courtroom together.

Had I been present during the reading of your dissent this morning I would proudly have shed another tear as I am shedding more than one now as I sit at my computer listening to news reports and reading your powerful words.

Thank you for your eloquence, wisdom, judgment, strength and courage. GOODY

Letter from Thurgood Marshall Jr. to
Justice Stephen G. Breyer (June 26, 2007).

Breaking the Promise of Brown

I had the privilege of serving as one of Justice Breyer's law clerks the year the Resegregation Cases were decided. Serving as a law clerk and—along with my fellow clerks, Jaren Casazza, Justin Driver, Tacy Flint, and Stephen Shackelford—assisting with the preparation of Justice Breyer's dissent in the Resegregation Cases remains the honor of a lifetime.

No introduction can convey Justice Breyer's even-handed appraisal of the law, the care with which he excavates the local histories in Seattle and Louisville that led to the legal controversy, or the deliberate arc of an argument aimed at those with open minds. This dissent was not designed to provide ammunition for like-minded allies or agitate those who vehemently disagreed, though it likely did both. It was meant to convince people of good faith, an audience seeking guidance on the uniquely American project of forming "a more perfect Union," that racial integration in public schools was not merely compatible with that noble aspiration and our Constitution—it was essential to both.

This introduction will honor that objective. It will first trace the critical sequence of Supreme Court decisions from *Brown v. Board of Education* (1954) to *Milliken v. Bradley* (1972) to the Resegregation Cases (2007) to explain the slow rise and current regression in school integration. Next is a synopsis of the structure and thrust of Justice Breyer's dissent, highlighting three of its most consequential features. This is followed by an accounting of why this topic matters so much—to Justice Breyer, to the political independence and perceived integrity of the Court, and to the future of public schools and race relations in America.

Understanding the context of these issues has never been more imperative. The images of our country these past few years—white supremacists draped in Confederate flags breaching the Capitol, racially charged violence in Charlottesville, protestors of police brutality enduring tear gas in Portland, marchers tearing down symbols of colonization and the Confederacy in Baltimore—are not only about the murders of George Floyd, Ahmaud Arbery, and countless others. Today's injustices are also the rotten harvest of a nation where Black children shiver in city classrooms with no heat, where suburban teenagers wear blackface and white robes for Halloween, and where too many parents everywhere look the other way.

Our generation's campaign against suffocating, enduring injustices does not end in our nation's classrooms, but it must begin there. As Justice Marshall wrote a half-century ago, "For unless our children begin to learn together, there is little hope that our people will ever learn to live together."[7]

SEGREGATION IN AMERICA'S SCHOOLS

School integration has stagnated in every corner of the country. Some of our biggest states—New York, California, Texas, which combine to account for nearly 30 percent of total public school enrollment—face the most daunting challenges. In New York, nearly two-thirds of Black students can be found at 90 to 100 percent minority schools. Likewise, more than half of all Latino students in California, New York, and Texas attend schools that are just as intensely segregated.

But segregation today is not confined to large states, or to the deep South for that matter. Sandwiched between New York, Illinois, and California, Maryland ranks as the third most segregated state for Black students, with 53 percent of Black chil-

7. *Milliken v. Bradley*, 418 U.S. 717, 783 (1974) (Marshall, J., dissenting).

dren attending 90 to 100 percent minority schools, many in the hypersegregated schools of Baltimore City. Similarly, almost half of all Latino students in New Jersey attend such schools, placing it fourth nationwide.

Most disturbing is that America's schools overall are as segregated today as they were fifty years ago. By 2011, the percentage of Black students in majority-white schools had returned to exactly where it was in 1968. Since then, it has only further declined to a record low of 19 percent in 2018, a pronounced drop to half the high-water mark of integration in 1988, when nearly 37 percent of Black students attended majority-white schools.

Back then, at the apex of integration, only 6 percent of America's public schools had virtually no white students. The backslide has been stark. In the quarter-century since 1988, that percentage has tripled to over 18 percent. In absolute numbers, the resegregation of the nation's school system has produced 4,000 more schools than there were in 1988 that are essentially devoid of white students (that is, schools with less than 1 percent white populations). To confess in 2022 that the late 1980s were the pinnacle of integration in America is to admit an epic national failure.

Responsibility for these disheartening trends lies at least partly with the Supreme Court. More than any other organ of government, the Court has defined the progress and retreat of school integration in America. At the start, it was the Court that, through its decisions, validated both the Civil Rights Act of 1964 and the enforcement activity of the Justice Department's Office of Civil Rights in the years that followed. The timeline marked by the Court's major decisions can be loosely divided into five intervals: (1) pre-1954, when the Court allowed overt de jure school segregation laws at the state and local level; (2) 1954–1968, a time of convulsion and noncompliance as local jurisdictions disregarded the Court's pronouncements beginning with *Brown*; (3) 1968–1974, a period of substantial desegregation propelled by strong federal decrees; (4) 1974–1988, a longer phase of more modest integration supported by weaker court orders as the Court gradually withdrew from the business of supervising school assignment policies; followed by (5) 1988 to the present, a period of steady resegregation as longstanding desegregation decrees were systematically dissolved.

So, how did we get from the clear-throated consensus of *Brown* to the division and acrimony coursing through the Resegregation Cases?

It was May 17, 1954, when the Supreme Court unanimously announced in *Brown v. Board of Education* that "separate educational facilities are inherently unequal," and, a year later, when it directed school districts to desegregate with "all deliberate speed."[8]

Rare in American history has a decision with so much promise met with such resistance. Emblematic of the times was the open insurrection that unfolded in Little Rock, Arkansas. Three years after *Brown*, standing on the doorstep of integration, Governor Orval Faubus ordered the Arkansas National Guard to block nine Black children from entering Little Rock Central High School. Interceding to "avoid anarchy," President Dwight Eisenhower federalized the National Guard to remove it from the governor's control and dispatched the 101st Airborne Division to integrate the school. An elite brigade of paratroopers took Black children by their hands and escorted them past mobs of protestors, all to comply with a Supreme Court decision that the governor of Arkansas was prepared to disregard.

---

8. *Brown v. Board of Education II*, 349 U.S. 294 (1955).

Breaking the Promise of Brown

In *Cooper v. Aaron* (1958), the dramatic standoff reached the Supreme Court. Just as it had in *Brown*, the Court issued another *per curiam* decision—an unsigned opinion adopted by all nine justices—unequivocally reaffirming that states were bound by *Brown* and that "no state legislator or executive or judicial officer can war against the Constitution without violating his undertaking to support it."[9]

The clash in Little Rock was a sign of the times. Resistance nationwide was no less fervent than what Black schoolchildren encountered in Arkansas, and little changed in most places until the late 1960s, when the Court lost patience with delay. In a series of intrepid decisions, the Supreme Court ordered the immediate dismantling of segregated schools, "root and branch," in Virginia in 1968,[10] struck down inadequate school choice plans that failed to achieve integration in Mississippi in 1969,[11] and authorized courts to impose busing plans and reconfigure school attendance zones to remedy past discrimination in North Carolina in 1971.[12] Federal desegregation decrees proliferated in the years that followed, producing meaningful integration in many parts of the country, including the deep South.

Unfortunately, far-reaching changes in where people lived counteracted the moral leadership of the Supreme Court and curbed the magnitude and pace of integration. Five million African Americans left the South beginning in 1940, and 80 percent of America's Black population lived in cities by 1970.[13] At the

9. *Cooper v. Aaron,* 358 U.S. 1, 18 (1958).

10. *Green v. County School Board of New Kent County,* 391 U.S. 430 (1968).

11. *Alexander v. Holmes County Bd. of Ed.,* 396 U.S. 19 (1969).

12. *Swann v. Charlotte-Mecklenburg Bd. of Ed.,* 402 U.S. 1 (1971); *Keyes v. School District No. 1, Denver,* 413 U.S. 189 (1973).

13. United States Census, "The Great Migration 1910–1970," www.census.gov/dataviz/visualizations/020/.

Soldiers from the 101st Airborne Division escort
African American students to Central High School
in Little Rock in September 1957, after the governor
of Arkansas tried to enforce segregation.

(*Source:* National Archives. Operation Arkansas, U.S. Army)

Little Rock, August 20, 1959. Rally in the state capital
to protest the integration of Central High School.

(*Source:* Library of Congress, *U.S. News & World
Report* Magazine Photograph Collection)

same time as African Americans arrived in urban centers to find jobs, buy homes, and raise families, millions of whites left for the suburbs, their departure only hastened by federal transportation policy, mortgage lending practices and redlining, and, for many, the specter of integrated schools.

Federal courts were ready to refashion desegregation decrees to account for these tectonic shifts in demographics. Detroit, for example, was one of many school districts facing the vexing challenge of suburbs with swelling white populations and a city of predominately Black students. Prompted by an NAACP lawsuit, a federal court crafted an interdistrict desegregation plan that combined students and schools across the city as well as the suburbs. The trial court concluded that an alternate plan limited to Detroit alone was inadequate and that the state of Michigan, not just the city of Detroit, was responsible for the unconstitutional conditions leading to schools segregated by race. Michigan Governor William Milliken appealed.

In *Milliken v. Bradley* (1974), the Supreme Court had a chance to ratify the district court's commonsense solution to achieve meaningful integration. It chose to construct a further roadblock instead. In a pivotal 5-4 decision, the Court ruled that suburbs shouldered no responsibility for segregation in city schools: "Where the schools of only one district have been affected, there is no constitutional power in the courts to decree relief balancing the racial composition of that district's schools with those of the surrounding districts."[14] To exonerate Michigan and relieve it of any responsibility for producing a remedy,

14. *Milliken v. Bradley*, 418 U.S. 717, 749 (1974).

the Court's majority closed its eyes to the federal district court's conclusion that Detroit's segregated schools were the direct product of a series of decisions by the state of Michigan.

Justice Thurgood Marshall, who as a lawyer had represented the winning side in *Brown*, feared that striking down the federal decree in Detroit would leave the district powerless to pursue integration in the face of white flight to the suburbs, a hurdle that was hardly unique to Detroit. The controversy provoked one of Justice Marshall's most commanding dissents. Sadly, nearly fifty years later, its sentiment and stirring words still ring true:

> We deal here with the right of all of our children, whatever their race, to an equal start in life and to an equal opportunity to reach their full potential as citizens. Those children who have been denied that right in the past deserve better than to see fences thrown up to deny them that right in the future.

> Desegregation is not and was never expected to be an easy task. Racial attitudes ingrained in our Nation's childhood and adolescence are not quickly thrown aside in its middle years. But just as the inconvenience of some cannot be allowed to stand in the way of the rights of others, so public opposition, no matter how strident, cannot be permitted to divert this Court from the enforcement of the constitutional principles at issue in this case.

Today's holding, I fear, is more a reflection of a perceived public mood that we have gone far enough in enforcing the Constitution's guarantee of equal justice than it is the product of neutral principles of law. In the short run, it may seem to be the easier course to allow our great metropolitan areas to be divided up each into two cities—one white, the other black—but it is a course, I predict, our people will ultimately regret. I dissent.[15]

Milliken reflected the fact that honest efforts to integrate schools were up against momentous trends that would defeat the ingenuity of school boards and courts alike. Justice Marshall worried that depriving federal courts of even the option of interdistrict solutions would drain the judiciary's power to the point of futility.

Despite the repercussions of *Milliken*, federal courts—albeit with their wings now clipped—refused to abandon the project of integration, and desegregation decrees continued to make some difference. Compared to the ten years of steady integration preceding *Milliken*, however, progress slowed considerably over the next decade. And America's schools would never be more integrated than 1988, when a wrenching reversal began.

The resegregation of America's schools began in earnest in the early 1990s. Around that time, in a trilogy of cases—in 1991, 1992, and 1995[16]—the Supreme Court materially lowered the standard for ending desegregation orders, making it easier than ever for courts to rule that school integration had come

15. *Milliken v. Bradley*, 418 U.S. 717, 814–15 (1974) (Marshall, J., dissenting).

16. See *Board of Educ. of Oklahoma City Public Schools v. Dowell*, 498 U.S. 237 (1991); *Freeman v. Pitts*, 503 U.S. 467 (1992); *Missouri v. Jenkins*, 515 U.S. 70 (1995).

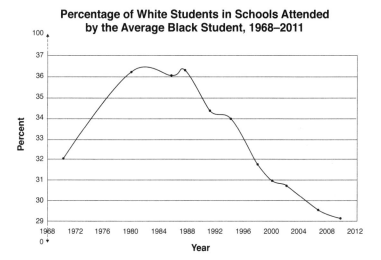

Percentage of White Students in Schools Attended by the Average Black Student, 1968–2011

Source: Erica Frankenberg, Jongyeon Ee, Jennifer B. Ayscue, and Gary Orfield, *Harming Our Common Future: America's Segregated Schools 65 Years After Brown*, May 10, 2019, Civil Rights Project and the Center for Education and Civil Rights.

far enough. Civil rights leader Julian Bond once warned, "The greatest impediment to achieving racial equality is the narcotic belief that we already have."[17] The 1990s and 2000s exemplified his admonition, as one federal court after another lifted desegregation decrees on the grounds that school districts had reached "unitary status" and that integration, as far as could be expected, had been accomplished. Nothing was further from the truth, and the fragile progress to date was in mortal jeopardy. By 2001, when President George W. Bush took office, there were just 600 school districts that were still subject to federal desegregation orders, a number that further dwindled to 380 by the end of his second term.

Such was the history inherited by the Supreme Court in 2007, when the next pivotal school segregation question would come before it. It was a history punctuated by bold pronouncements like *Brown* and *Cooper* only to see the gains inspired by them compromised and recede.

Looking back across the decades, it is easier to catalog the impact of the individual victories and setbacks. From 1954, when *Brown* was decided until the late 1960s, there was little adherence to the mandate of integration. In the late 1960s and early 1970s, the Court's increasingly impatient directives to desegregate generated momentum. In 1974, however, the Court's divided ruling in *Milliken*, refusing to tackle the obstacle of white flight, flattened the pace of integration, which, remarkably, peaked in 1988. This is when the resegregation phase commenced, as the Supreme Court loosened its own standards, allowing school districts to untangle themselves from the federal decrees that had until then propelled integration forward.

17. Speech of Julian Bond, Lyndon B. Johnson School of Public Affairs, The University of Texas at Austin (January 28, 2015).

Like in 1974, when the Court was confronted with the problem of suburban white flight, the Court had a chance in 2007 to reckon with the resegregation of America's schools. By then, local school districts were choosing to battle resegregation on their own, often voluntarily undertaking the very strategies they had previously been compelled by federal courts to adopt. The Supreme Court was asked simply not to stand in their way.

THE RESEGREGATION CASES

The very school districts that once spurned integration now strive for it. The long history of their efforts reveals the complexities and difficulties they have faced. And in light of those challenges, they have asked us not to take from their hands the instruments they have used to rid their schools of racial segregation, instruments that they believe are needed to overcome the problems of cities divided by race and poverty.[18]

As federal courts dissolved desegregation decrees and city-to-suburb population shifts continued, school districts across America struggled to cope with the resegregation of public schools. Some school systems affirmatively fought resegregation even without the formal spur of a federal court order. The central question that came before the Supreme Court in the Resegregation Cases arose from two such districts in Seattle, Washington, and Louisville, Kentucky.

Both had a long history of segregated schools reinforced by state policy and had faced civil rights lawsuits in the past—in

18. *Parents Involved in Community Schools v. Seattle School District No. 1,* 551 U.S. 701, 868 (2007) (Breyer, J., dissenting).

17

Louisville's case resulting in a remedial decree that was not dissolved until 2000. Both made progress but remained frustrated by mounting racial imbalance in their public schools. In Seattle, officials adopted a school choice program that, for the sake of creating high schools that reflected the racial diversity of the district, took account of a student's race in a narrow set of cases. The Louisville school district—also for the purpose of integrating its schools—simply reinstituted the same elementary school assignment plan it had originally been compelled to adopt when it was under a federal order.

In both cities, students ranked their school preferences and, in some instances, the districts took account of the race of the student and the composition of the school to ensure that student assignments did not exacerbate already segregated schools. Parents whose students were assigned to schools other than their top choices sued. Federal trial and appellate courts rejected those challenges and declared both programs lawful.

The Supreme Court agreed to review these decisions. Oral argument was held in December 2006, and the Court announced its decision on June 28, 2007, the last day of the first full term after Chief Justice John Roberts and Justice Samuel Alito joined the Court. Just as President Richard Nixon's appointments of Justices Lewis Powell and William Rehnquist in December 1971 made the difference in the 5-4 decision in *Milliken* in 1974, so too did President George W. Bush's appointments of Chief Justice Roberts (2005) and Justice Alito (2006) prove decisive in the Resegregation Cases of 2007.

Chief Justice Roberts, joined by Justices Antonin Scalia, Clarence Thomas, and Alito, announced the judgment of the Court. He wrote that, because the school district programs took explicit account of race, they violated the Equal Protection Clause of the Constitution, no matter the severity of public school segregation or the claimed righteousness of the districts' purpose to eradicate it: "The way to stop discrimination on the basis of race is to stop discriminating on the basis of race."[19]

Justice Anthony Kennedy supplied the pivotal fifth vote to strike down the plans. While he accepted that combating resegregation was a laudable objective and would constitute a "compelling state interest," he nevertheless found that Seattle's and Louisville's plans were not "narrowly tailored" enough.[20] It did not matter to Justice Kennedy that the current plans resembled plans that the districts had previously used, sometimes under the mandate of a federal court.

Justice Stevens joined Justice Breyer's dissent "in its entirety," calling it "eloquent and unanswerable."[21] He added a short, separate dissent that took aim at the Chief Justice's sloganeering, dismantling the Chief Justice's confidence that "the way to stop discrimination . . . is to stop discriminating"[22]:

> This sentence reminds me of Anatole France's observation: "[T]he majestic equality of the la[w], forbid[s] rich and poor alike to sleep under bridges, to beg in the streets, and to steal their bread." The Chief Justice fails to note that it was only Black schoolchildren who were so ordered; indeed, the history books do not tell stories of white children struggling to attend Black schools. In

19. *Parents Involved in Community Schools v. Seattle School District No. 1*, 551 U.S. 701, 748 (2007).
20. *Id.*, at 789 (Kennedy, J., concurring in part and concurring in the judgment).
21. *Id.*, at 798 (Stevens, J., dissenting).
22. *Id.*, at 748.

this and other ways, the Chief Justice rewrites the history of one of this Court's most important decisions.[23]

Justice Stevens, the longest-serving justice then on the Court, ended with a reminder of how dramatic and indefensible a departure the majority's decision was: "It is my firm conviction that no Member of the Court I joined in 1975 would have agreed with today's decision."[24]

The principal dissent was penned by Justice Stephen Breyer. His impassioned, seventy-seven-page dissent in the Resegregation Cases marks a conspicuous departure in tone and length from his other opinions.

Part I of the dissent—titled, simply, "Facts"—begins with a thorough history of school integration initiatives in Seattle and Louisville, chronicling "the extensive and ongoing efforts of two school districts to bring about greater racial integration of their public schools." With each successive attempt, both cities sought to rely more upon school choice, to depend less upon racial classifications, and to saddle families with fewer burdens. The stories of Seattle and Louisville—typical of the sagas of so many American cities—illustrate "the complexity of the tasks and the practical difficulties that local school boards face when they seek to achieve greater racial integration."

With this history in focus, in Part II ("The Legal Standard"), Justice Breyer surveys the law, reciting an unbroken line of Supreme Court, federal appellate, and state court decisions faithful to *Brown*. This part draws its strength from *Swann v. Charlotte-Mecklenburg Bd. of Ed.* (1971), where a unanimous Supreme Court said that school authorities were entitled to take

23. *Id.*, at 799 (Stevens, J., dissenting).
24. *Id.*, at 803 (Stevens, J., dissenting).

explicit account of race to prepare children of different races to learn and live together:

> School authorities are traditionally charged with broad power to formulate and implement educational policy and might well conclude, for example, that in order to prepare students to live in a pluralistic society each school should have a prescribed ratio of Negro to white students reflecting the proportion for the district as a whole. To do this as an educational policy is within the broad discretionary powers of school authorities.[25]

For Justice Breyer, this was controlling precedent, and evidence of *Swann*'s vitality was everywhere: it had "been accepted by every branch of government," underpinning numerous state court decisions, presidential orders, and acts of Congress. Justice Breyer further explains that this unwavering history, rooted in constitutional amendments "designed to make citizens of slaves," supported a "careful review" of the districts' plans, but not the kind of "strict scrutiny" reserved for policies meant to divide rather than unite people by race.

Even though a more relaxed constitutional test was appropriate, in Part III ("Applying the Legal Standard"), Justice Breyer nonetheless concludes that plans to combat resegregation in Seattle and Louisville also survive the more exacting standard of "strict scrutiny." Generally, to pass strict scrutiny, the government must show a "compelling state interest" and establish that its method is "narrowly tailored" to achieve that interest.

In Justice Breyer's estimation, achieving racially integrated

25. *Swann v. Charlotte-Mecklenburg Bd. of Ed.*, 402 U.S. 1, 16 (1971).

public schools constitutes a compelling state interest (a conclusion shared by Justice Kennedy). He explains that inclusive schools combine three critical interests—remedial, educational, and democratic. First, integration honors a pledge to set right the damage of "America's heresies,"[26] from the modern vestiges of past segregation back to the original sins of slavery and Black Codes and Jim Crow laws. Second, schools are entitled to seek the kind of classroom diversity they believe will produce superior academic outcomes for all children. Finally, bringing together children of different races to learn and cooperate with one another is perhaps the best hope to make of "a land of three hundred million people one Nation."[27] For Justice Breyer, if a governmental interest that unites "these three elements is not 'compelling,' what is?"[28]

Next, to prove the plans were narrowly tailored, Justice Breyer compares them to past desegregation plans and to the affirmative action admissions policy at the University of Michigan Law School,[29] all of which the Supreme Court had previously approved. Neither Seattle nor Louisville used impermissible racial quotas (which the Court's precedent had forbidden) but, instead, looked to race only as a starting point. The predominant factor for student assignment in both cities was not race but student choice. And the plans were literally tailored over time, as each school district experimented and innovated based on its experiences, with vanishing use of forced busing, greater reliance upon school choice, and less severe consequences than rejection from Michigan's flagship law school.

Justice Breyer reminds us that countless school districts have

26. Ta-Nehisi Coates, *Between the World and Me* (2015), 6.
27. *Parents Involved in Community Schools v. Seattle School District No. 1*, 551 U.S. 701, 840 (2007) (Breyer, J., dissenting).
28. *Id.*, at 843 (Breyer, J., dissenting).
29. See *Grutter v. Bollinger*, 539 U.S. 306 (2003).

used more "explicitly race-conscious methods, including mandatory busing"[30] to achieve integration than the plans under attack. At the same time, he challenges the majority to find a single example from anywhere in American history of a school district that fought off resegregation relying on a less race-conscious plan: "Nothing in the extensive history of desegregation efforts over the past 50 years gives the districts, or this Court, any reason to believe that another method is possible to accomplish these goals."[31]

After thirty-three pages of meticulous analysis in Parts II and III, Justice Breyer, in Part IV ("Direct Precedent"), reinforces his legal conclusions by simple reference to controlling precedents that dealt directly with desegregation plans in Louisville and Seattle.[32] On the basis of these prior rulings, Justice Breyer firmly rebuked the majority's decision, which, in the name of equal protection, invalidated plans that the previous day the Constitution appeared to require:

> Yesterday, the plans under review were lawful. Today, they are not. Yesterday, the citizens of this Nation could look for guidance to this Court's unanimous pronouncements concerning desegregation. Today, they cannot. Yesterday, school boards had available to them a full range of means to combat segregated schools. Today, they do not.[33]

30. *Parents Involved in Community Schools v. Seattle School District No. 1*, 551 U.S. 701, 850 (2007) (Breyer, J., dissenting).

31. *Id.*, at 851–52 (Breyer, J., dissenting).

32. See *Hampton v. Jefferson Cty. Bd. of Ed.*, 102 F.Supp.2d 358 (WD Ky. 2000); *Washington v. Seattle School Dist. No. 1*, 458 U.S. 457 (1982).

33. *Parents Involved in Community Schools v. Seattle School District No. 1*, 551 U.S. 701, 865–66 (2007) (Breyer, J., dissenting).

In Part V ("Consequences"), the dissent outlines the practical fallout of the Court's ruling. A constitutional pragmatist, Justice Breyer pays attention to what the Court's decisions mean for those charged with the day-to-day responsibilities of administering local schools. He warns of the decision's dire impact on local efforts to come to grips with inequities of race and class in America's schools. Guided by a review of hundreds of desegregation plans from all over the country, addressing different kinds of local challenges, each with distinct elements, most with explicit race-conscious features, Justice Breyer urges judicial humility:

> I do not claim to know how best to stop harmful discrimination; how best to create a society that includes all Americans; how best to overcome our serious problems of increasing *de facto* segregation, troubled inner city schooling, and poverty correlated with race. But, as a judge, I do know that the Constitution does not authorize judges to dictate solutions to these problems. Rather, the Constitution creates a democratic political system through which the people themselves must together find answers. And it is for them to debate how best to educate the Nation's children and how best to administer America's schools to achieve that aim. The Court should leave them to their work.[34]

Justice Breyer then closes the dissent of his career with a poignant reflection about the legacy of the Supreme Court's most celebrated decision:

34. *Id.*, at 862 (Breyer, J., dissenting).

Finally, what of the hope and promise of *Brown*? For much of this Nation's history, the races remained divided. It was not long ago that people of different races drank from separate fountains, rode on separate buses, and studied in separate schools. In this Court's finest hour, *Brown v. Board of Education* challenged this history and helped to change it. For *Brown* held out a promise. It was a promise embodied in three Amendments designed to make citizens of slaves. It was the promise of true racial equality—not as a matter of fine words on paper, but as a matter of everyday life in the Nation's cities and schools. It was about the nature of a democracy that must work for all Americans. It sought one law, one Nation, one people, not simply as a matter of legal principle but in terms of how we actually live.[35]

With the unmistakable echo of Justice Marshall's closing in *Milliken*, Justice Breyer ends:

The last half-century has witnessed great strides toward racial equality, but we have not yet realized the promise of *Brown*. To invalidate the plans under review is to threaten the promise of *Brown*. The plurality's position, I fear, would break that promise. This is a decision that the Court and the Nation will come to regret.

I must dissent.[36]

Justice Breyer's dissent is built upon an edifice of local history, a faithful application of firm precedent, a candid appraisal

35. *Id.*, at 867–68 (Breyer, J., dissenting).
36. *Id.*, at 868 (Breyer, J., dissenting).

of the decision's practical consequences, and an appreciation of what it ultimately will mean for the nation's fundamental aspiration to unite a divided people.

CHALLENGING LEGAL CONVENTION

If Justice Breyer's first audience is the American people and history is his second, law professors and the next generation of law students are, no doubt, his third. Contained in Justice Breyer's dissent are three steel-toed challenges to judicial orthodoxies that are usually just a topic of scholarly discourse.

First, Justice Breyer challenges the "distinction between *de jure* segregation (caused by school systems) and *de facto* segregation (caused, *e.g.*, by housing patterns or generalized societal discrimination)," explaining that this difference is "meaningless in the present context."[37] When a court encounters *de jure* segregation—segregation by law—it enjoys virtually limitless latitude to fashion an appropriate remedy. Yet courts are thought to have no authority to rectify *de facto* segregation. For Justice Breyer, it is impractical and unwise to rest the scope of a federal court's power to redress inequity upon such an academic, elusive determination.

In Seattle, for instance, schools may not have been segregated by law, strictly speaking, but Black children were kept apart from white children by school boundary lines fixed by the school district. Thus, state policies bluntly produced segregation in Seattle just as much as laws directly segregated schools in other places. The city of Seattle admitted as much, voluntarily

37. *Id.*, at 806 (Breyer, J., dissenting).

desegregating its schools without a court order when its policies were challenged as *de jure* segregation by private plaintiffs. In that regard, the presence or absence of a judicial order predicated on *de jure* segregation cannot be dispositive either, since numerous school districts avoided a federal decree by conceding that their policies caused racially segregated schools. According to Justice Breyer, because a distinction between segregation in law and segregation in fact cannot be neatly drawn given the cluttered, chaotic history of America's racist policies, this imagined distinction should not dictate what remedies are available to address the nation's failures.

Second, Justice Breyer contests the common impression that courts are wholly free to brush aside "dicta," no matter the legacy or character of that dicta. Dicta are those passages in a prior decision that are informative or explanatory but are not "necessary" to a court's ruling. Such language is typically treated as extraneous, editorial commentary that may guide a court's analysis but does not control the outcome of future cases.

In his dissent, Justice Breyer makes clear his view that all dicta are not equal. In *Swann*, Chief Justice Warren Burger explains that race-conscious school policies designed to promote integration and prepare students to live in a diverse country were, undoubtedly, "within the broad discretionary powers of school authorities."[38] The claim was not controversial at the time, and the pronouncement was technically dicta—meaning it was not required to reach the result in *Swann*. For years, however, public agencies and state and federal courts relied on Chief Justice Burger's statement to resolve numerous cases. *Swann* had been affirmed by contemporary and subsequent Supreme

---

38. *Swann v. Charlotte-Mecklenburg Bd. of Ed.*, 402 U.S. 1, 16 (1971).

Court pronouncements,[39] as well as by numerous state courts that adopted the logic of *Swann* before and after it was decided.

Swann was, thus, no different than Justice Lewis Powell's concurring opinion in the 1978 affirmative action case, *Regents of the University of California v. Bakke.*[40] Justice Powell's opinion was also technically dicta but provided decades of guidance for university administrators across the nation as they sought to craft constitutionally sound affirmative action admissions policies. For Justice Breyer dicta could harden into widespread judicial consensus and should, then, carry the controlling weight of precedent. To give the pedantic label "dicta" the talismanic power to strip a court's pronouncement of its authority is to ignore how the law develops, how judicial wisdom and reasoning fortifies itself, and how courts operate in the real world.

Finally, Justice Breyer attacks the central plank of Chief Justice Robert's legal analysis, that any measure that takes account of race should be treated with the highest degree of suspicion, regardless of whether the goal is to divide the races or to bring them together. This mechanical approach to the law of equal protection is not just overly simplistic—for Justice Breyer, it also contradicts the origins and purpose of the Fourteenth Amendment of the U.S. Constitution:

> The Amendment sought to bring into American society as full members those whom the Nation had previously held in slavery. . . . There is reason to believe that those who drafted an Amendment with this basic purpose in

39. *North Carolina Bd. of Ed. v. Swann*, 402 U. S. 43 (1971); *Bustop, Inc. v. Los Angeles Bd. of Ed.*, 439 U. S. 1380 (1978).
40. *Regents of the University of California v. Bakke*, 438 U.S. 265 (1978).

mind would have understood the legal and practical difference between the use of race-conscious criteria in defiance of that purpose, namely to keep the races apart, and the use of race-conscious criteria to further that purpose, namely to bring the races together.[41]

In the case of Seattle and Louisville, the school choice plans were devised not to divide and separate the races but, rather, to bring schoolchildren of different races together. In Justice Breyer's view, while the Constitution "almost always forbids the former, it is significantly more lenient in respect to the latter."[42] After all, the promise of equal protection is rooted in the Fourteenth Amendment, which pledged equality to an emancipated race in a nation riven by civil war. A state or local government's efforts to deliver on that hallowed promise could not, in fidelity with the Constitution, be equated with measures undertaken to break it.

Whether it is the rigid taxonomy separating *de jure* and *de facto* segregation, the crude recitation of the difference between loose dicta and strict precedent, or the uniform treatment of all race-conscious policies no matter their aim, Justice Breyer refuses to reduce the subtle alchemy of decisionmaking in hard cases into a rote chemical formula. The Resegregation Cases confirm that Justice Breyer is foremost a practical jurist, not an abstract professor of theory. These cases exemplify how Justice Breyer approaches the role of the law and the work of the Court. For him, Supreme Court decisions are not political, academic, or polemical exercises. At their best, they grapple with the na-

41. *Parents Involved in Community Schools v. Seattle School District No. 1*, 551 U.S. 701, 829 (2007) (Breyer, J., dissenting).
42. *Id.*, at 830 (Breyer, J., dissenting).

tion's enduring failures and provide to a messy democracy both the clarity and the freedom it requires to permit "we the people" to govern ourselves.

THE POWER OF DISSENT

It is not often in the law that so few have so quickly changed so much.[43]

"Justice John Paul Stevens, Justice David Souter, Justice Ruth Bader Ginsburg and I dissent." With this conspicuously formal opening, so began Justice Breyer as he delivered from the bench his landmark opinion in the Resegregation Cases. Issuing a dissent from the bench is itself a rare event. It is a clarion signal that the divergence of opinion in the case is no ordinary disagreement, even among the fiercely contested controversies that reach the nation's highest court. Justice Breyer's stirring oration lasted twenty-two minutes, longer than any prior reading of a majority, concurring, or dissenting opinion, in Supreme Court history.

In the middle of Justice Breyer's recitation is a sentence that appears nowhere in his dissenting opinion, a rogue, uncharacteristic line that pierced the apolitical veneer of the Court: "It is not often in the law that so few have so quickly changed so much." Justice Breyer's seeming reference to the arrival of Chief Justice John Roberts and Justice Samuel Alito and the legal cataclysms they had wrought in a single term was more than commentary about the individual case at hand. For Justice Breyer, the abrupt abandonment of significant precedent threatened the Court's in-

43. Oral Opinion of Justice Breyer, *Parents Involved in Community Schools v. Seattle School District No. 1*, 551 U.S. 701 (2007) (No. 05-908), www.oyez.org/cases/2006/05-908.

stitutional legitimacy. It was a charged statement at the end of a term as divisive as any the Supreme Court had ever seen.

Of the seventy-three cases decided by the Court that year, a third of them—two dozen in total—ended in 5-4 splits, a greater proportion than any other term in modern history, before or since. In a substantial majority of those divided rulings, the same four justices (Stevens, Souter, Ginsburg, and Breyer) found themselves united in dissent. To place the October 2006 term in perspective, a decade later (the October 2016 term), there were only seven decisions that ended in 5-4 splits (10 percent).

What Justice Breyer feared most was the diminishment of the Court into just another political institution, no different than Congress or the presidency, defined by the popular trade winds of the moment. After all, if venerated legal precedent could vanish overnight with the arrival of a new presidential appointee, the Supreme Court becomes more an executive agency than an independent third branch of government. As Justice Breyer has articulated in speeches and writings over the years, the Court's legitimacy—the reason the country honors its decisions—depends on its independence and the public's confidence in its independence.

Justice Breyer often reminds audiences that, after *Worchester v. Georgia* in 1832, where the Supreme Court recognized the tribal sovereignty of the Cherokee, President Andrew Jackson bluntly challenged the Court's power to compel Georgia to honor its ruling. He reportedly said: "John Marshall has made his decision; now let him enforce it."[44] The tragedy of the Trail of Tears followed. A century later, *Cooper v. Aaron* (1958) doc-

44. Historians generally concur the memorable quotation is likely apocryphal, but it fairly reflected the view President Jackson shared in written correspondence soon after the Supreme Court's decision.

umented the open disdain of the governor of Arkansas after the Supreme Court's desegregation decisions. Deployment of the 101st Airborne Division was required to enforce those rulings.

Such measures, thankfully, are no longer needed. A jurist from another country once asked Justice Breyer, "Why do Americans do what the Court says?" Justice Breyer explained that it is our winding history, not any feature of our legal doctrine, that explains the rule of law in the United States:[45]

> Reflect for a moment upon how long it has taken for our Nation to learn the importance of the rule of law. Think of our ups and downs. Think of slavery. Think of a civil war. Think of eighty years of segregation. Out of those trying experiences and the many others that this Nation has endured, we have emerged with at least one substantial attainment: While we may not agree with the outcome of a particular case, we will follow the rule of law. And it is this fundamental belief that binds together our Nation of 300 million people.[46]

The cloak of legitimacy that America's struggles have conferred upon the Supreme Court should not be taken for granted. Should the faith of the American people in the political independence of the federal courts begin to fray, we risk returning to a time when the Court's pronouncements were only as valid as the weight of public sentiment supporting them.

In the context of school desegregation, this is not an abstract

45. Stephen G. Breyer, *Making Our Democracy Work: A Judge's View* (Vintage, 2011).

46. Stephen G. Breyer, "An Independent Judiciary: In Honor of the Sesquicentennial Anniversary of the Massachusetts Superior Court." Sept. 22, 2009, Fairmont Copley Plaza Hotel, Boston, MA.

fear. When two appointments by President Nixon changed the balance of power in 1971, the Court's commitment to desegregation shifted as well. Recall, in *Milliken*, Justice Marshall suspected the majority's decision was "more a reflection of a perceived public mood" than it was "the product of neutral principles of law."[47] More than fifty years later, as two new Justices straightaway bulldozed settled precedent in the Resegregation Cases, Justice Breyer, no doubt, heard the worrisome echo of that history.

Justice Breyer's concerns about the politicization of the Supreme Court are not confined to the Court's decisions alone. He surely appreciates that in the days of his appointment, the confirmation proceedings of Justices were far less fractious. Back then, the divided confirmation votes of Chief Justice William Rehnquist (65-33 in 1986) and Justice Clarence Thomas (52-48 in 1991) were notable exceptions. Justices were generally confirmed with the overwhelming support of the U.S. Senate: Justice John Paul Stevens (98-0, 1975), Justice Sandra Day O'Connor (99-0, 1981), Justice Antonin Scalia (98-0, 1986), Justice Anthony Kennedy (97-0, 1988), Justice David Souter (90-9, 1990), Justice Ruth Bader Ginsburg (96-3, 1993), and Justice Breyer (87-9, 1994).

After Justice Breyer's appointment, a full decade would pass before a new justice would join the Court. The arrival of Chief Justice John Roberts (78-22, 2005) and Justice Samuel Alito (58-42, 2006) marked the beginning of a far different era. Every successive appointment has produced a splintered Senate vote: Justice Sonia Sotomayor (68-31, 2009), Justice Elena Kagan (63-37, 2010), Justice Neil Gorsuch (54-45, 2017), Justice Brett Kavanaugh (50-48, 2018), and Justice Amy Coney Barrett (52-48, 2020).

It is almost hard to believe that Justices Stevens and Scalia,

47. See *Milliken v. Bradley*, 418 U.S. 717, 814 (1974) (Marshall, J., dissenting).

representing the right and left flanks of the Court, were unanimously confirmed. So, too, were Justices O'Connor and Kennedy, who, each in their time, controlled the center of the Court, casting the decisive vote in innumerable cases. They are the only two living justices—and they may very well be the last—who were confirmed by the Senate without a single vote cast against them.

Justices are stewards of the Constitution. They are also responsible for safeguarding the hard-earned authority of the Court itself. In this respect, Justice Breyer's dissent in the Resegregation Cases was not just about respecting legal precedent; it was also about preserving the Court's political independence and institutional integrity in the increasingly jaundiced eyes of the American public.

BREAKING THE PROMISE OF *BROWN*

Finally, what of the hope and promise of *Brown*? For much of this nation's history, the races remained divided. In this Court's finest hour, *Brown v. Board of Education* challenged this history and helped to change it.[48]

Above all, of course, the Resegregation Cases are about the fate of American schools. In his written opinion and in the solemn reading of his dissent, Justice Breyer warned of increasingly segregated schools, deteriorating educational outcomes, and a nation where the races remain divided. Tragically, the justice's worst fears continue to come true.

Nationwide school statistics mask the appalling reality in

48. *Parents Involved in Community Schools v. Seattle School District No. 1, 551* U.S. 701, 867 (2007) (Breyer, J., dissenting).

America, as, too often, statistics do. The numbers at individual schools tell an even more ominous story than the stunning but abstract fact that America's schools are more segregated today than they were in 1968.

Take my hometown of Baltimore. Of thirty-eight public high schools, all but four are over 90 percent minority; over half are 98 to 100 percent minority. None of these intensely segregated schools have an average SAT score above 1,000, with most of them hovering in the 700s and 800s. Each year, students at too many of these schools, between the ordinary gauntlet of homework, hormones, and sports practice, attend the funerals of classmates who have been senselessly gunned down before graduation. Seven such students at Francis M. Wood High School (Excel Academy) were killed in the span of fifteen months, five of them in a single school year (2016–2017).

The three schools with the highest test scores—Baltimore Polytechnic (Poly) (where my mother first taught in 1970), Baltimore School for the Arts (BSA), and Baltimore City College (City)—are also the most racially diverse, and each is a majority-minority school (that is, more than 50 percent minority). The best performing high school that is more than 90 percent minority is Western High School (where my father ended his decades-long teaching career at the age of eighty). With over 1,000 students, Western is the oldest all-girls public high school in America; it is also predominantly Black, with white students accounting for less than 5 percent of the student population. City, Poly, School for the Arts, and Western are the acclaimed exceptions to the struggles of Baltimore schools.

Frederick Douglass High School in West Baltimore, where my father also taught, is more typical. The student body at Douglass is 99 percent Black, and most classes have no white students at all. Only 70 percent of its students graduate, and the average SAT score—742—is among the lowest in the state. Its 900 students know they cannot drink from the water fountains, not because of their race but because the corroding pipes underneath them leech lead into the water supply. Students also know that some number of school days will be canceled each year because Douglass has no heat or air conditioning. Remarkably, the one enduring source of pride for the beleaguered school is that, in 1925, a young Black man in the top third of his class graduated from Douglass and went on to become the first African American justice on the United States Supreme Court.

I like to believe Justice Marshall would be proud that we continue to fight to make real the promise of *Brown*, that for so many of us its ambition remains noble and worthy. He would, no doubt, be ashamed, however, of the state of public schools in the nation today, beginning with his alma mater. He would be rightly outraged to see the vast resegregation that has occurred. And he would be furious to hear of the practical impediments the Supreme Court itself continues to erect, from the *Milliken* decision that prompted his dissent to the Resegregation Cases that inspired Justice Breyer's.

What would upset him most, I think, is the ignorance, vitriol, apprehension, and hate that still characterize so many of our racial divisions. It is exactly as he predicted: "For unless our children begin to learn together, there is little hope that our people will ever learn to live together."[49]

That was Justice Marshall's vision of democracy in America.

49. *Milliken v. Bradley*, 418 U.S. 717, 783 (1974) (Marshall, J., dissenting).

I firmly believe it is Justice Breyer's too. As Justice Breyer wrote in the closing passage of his dissent, the promise of *Brown v. Board of Education* was "about the nature of a democracy that must work for all Americans. It sought one law, one Nation, one people, not simply as a matter of legal principle but in terms of how we actually live."

Until segregation in America's schools is part of our history rather than our present—and even then, perhaps—the cautionary words of Justice Breyer in the Resegregation Cases should reverberate in classrooms across the country and in the hearts and minds of citizens and schoolchildren everywhere.

JUSTICE BREYER'S DISSENT

*Parents Involved in Community
Schools* v. *Seattle School District No. 1*
&
Meredith v. *Jefferson County
Board of Education*

551 U.S. 701 (2007)
Decided on June 28, 2007

JUSTICE BREYER, with whom JUSTICE STEVENS, JUSTICE SOUTER, and JUSTICE GINSBURG join, dissenting.

These cases consider the longstanding efforts of two local school boards to integrate their public schools. The school board plans before us resemble many others adopted in the last 50 years by primary and secondary schools throughout the Nation. All of those plans represent local efforts to bring about the kind of racially integrated education that *Brown v. Board of Education*,[1] long ago promised—efforts that this Court has repeatedly required, permitted, and encouraged local authorities to undertake. This Court has recognized that the public interests at stake in such cases are "compelling." We have approved of "narrowly tailored" plans that are no less race-conscious than the plans before us. And we have understood that the

Constitution *permits* local communities to adopt desegregation plans even where it does not *require* them to do so.

The plurality pays inadequate attention to this law, to past opinions' rationales, their language, and the contexts in which they arise. As a result, it reverses course and reaches the wrong conclusion. In doing so, it distorts precedent, it misapplies the relevant constitutional principles, it announces legal rules that will obstruct efforts by state and local governments to deal effectively with the growing resegregation of public schools, it threatens to substitute for present calm a disruptive round of race-related litigation, and it undermines *Brown*'s promise of integrated primary and secondary education that local communities have sought to make a reality. This cannot be justified in the name of the Equal Protection Clause.

I

Facts

The historical and factual context in which these cases arise is critical. In *Brown*, this Court held that the government's segregation of schoolchildren by race violates the Constitution's promise of equal protection. The Court emphasized that "education is perhaps the most important function of state and local governments."[2] And it thereby set the Nation on a path toward public school integration.

In dozens of subsequent cases, this Court told school districts previously segregated by law what they must do at a minimum to comply with *Brown*'s constitutional holding. The measures required by those cases often included race-conscious practices, such as mandatory busing and race-based restrictions on voluntary transfers.[3]

Beyond those minimum requirements, the Court left much of the determination of how to achieve integration to the judgment of local communities. Thus, in respect to race-conscious desegregation measures that the Constitution *permitted,* but did not *require* (measures similar to those at issue here), this Court unanimously stated:

> "School authorities are traditionally charged with broad power to formulate and implement educational policy and might well conclude, for example, that in order to prepare students to live in a pluralistic society each school should have a prescribed ratio of Negro to white students reflecting the proportion for the district as a whole. *To do this as an educational policy is within the broad discretionary powers of school authorities.*"[4]

As a result, different districts—some acting under court decree, some acting in order to avoid threatened lawsuits, some seeking to comply with federal administrative orders, some acting purely voluntarily, some acting after federal courts had dissolved earlier orders—adopted, modified, and experimented with hosts of different kinds of plans, including race-conscious plans, all with a similar objective: greater racial integration of public schools.[5] The techniques that different districts have employed range "from voluntary transfer programs to mandatory reassignment."[6] And the design of particular plans has been "dictated by both the law and the specific needs of the district."[7]

Overall these efforts brought about considerable racial integration. More recently, however, progress has stalled. Between 1968 and 1980, the number of black children attending a school where minority children constituted more than half of the school fell from 77% to 63% in the Nation (from 81% to 57% in the South) but then reversed direction by the year 2000, rising from 63% to 72% in the Nation (from 57% to 69% in the South). Similarly, between 1968 and 1980, the number of black children attending schools that were more than 90% minority fell from 64% to 33% in the Nation (from 78% to 23% in the South), but that too reversed direction, rising by the year 2000 from 33% to 37% in the Nation (from 23% to 31% in the South). As of 2002, almost 2.4 million students, or over 5% of all public school enrollment, attended schools with a white population of less than 1%. Of these, 2.3 million were black and Latino students, and only 72,000 were white. Today, more than one in six black children attend a school that is 99–100% minority.[8] In light of the evident risk of a return to school systems that are in fact (though not in law) resegregated, many school districts have felt a need to maintain or to extend their integration efforts.

The upshot is that myriad school districts operating in myriad circumstances have devised myriad plans, often with race-conscious elements, all for the sake of eradicating earlier school segregation, bringing about integration, or preventing retrogression. Seattle and Louisville are two such districts, and the histories of their present plans set forth typical school integration stories.

I describe those histories at length in order to highlight three important features of these cases. First, the school districts' plans serve "compelling interests" and are "narrowly tailored" on any reasonable definition of those terms. Second, the distinction between *de jure* segregation (caused by school systems) and *de facto* segregation (caused, *e.g.*, by housing patterns or generalized societal discrimination) is meaningless in the present context, thereby dooming the plurality's endeavor to find support for its views in that distinction. Third, real-world efforts to substitute racially diverse for racially segregated schools (however caused) are complex, to the point where the Constitution cannot plausibly be interpreted to rule out categorically all local efforts to use means that are "conscious" of the race of individuals.

In both Seattle and Louisville, the local school districts began with schools that were highly segregated in fact. In both cities plaintiffs filed lawsuits claiming unconstitutional segregation. In Louisville, a federal district court found that school segregation reflected pre-*Brown* state laws separating the races. In Seattle, the plaintiffs alleged that school segregation unconstitutionally reflected not only generalized societal discrimination and residential housing patterns, but also *school board policies and actions* that had helped to create, maintain, and aggravate racial segregation. In Louisville, a federal court entered a remedial decree. In Seattle, the parties settled after the school district pledged to undertake a desegregation plan. In both cities, the school boards adopted plans designed to achieve integration by bringing about more racially diverse schools. In each city the school board modified its plan several times in light of, for example, hostility to busing, the threat of resegregation, and the desirability of introducing greater student choice. And in each city, the school boards' plans have evolved over time in ways that progressively *diminish* the plans' use of explicit race-conscious criteria.

The histories that follow set forth these basic facts. They

are based upon numerous sources, which for ease of exposition I have cataloged, along with their corresponding citations, at Appendix B, *infra*.

A
Seattle

1. *Segregation, 1945 to 1956.* During and just after World War II, significant numbers of black Americans began to make Seattle their home. Few black residents lived outside the central section of the city. Most worked at unskilled jobs. Although black students made up about 3% of the total Seattle population in the mid-1950s, nearly all black children attended schools where a majority of the population was minority. Elementary schools in central Seattle were between 60% and 80% black; Garfield, the central district high school, was more than 50% minority; schools outside the central and southeastern sections of Seattle were virtually all white.

2. *Preliminary Challenges, 1956 to 1969.* In 1956, a memo for the Seattle School Board reported that school segregation reflected not only segregated housing patterns but also school board policies that permitted white students to transfer out of black schools while restricting the transfer of black students into white schools. In 1958, black parents whose children attended Harrison Elementary School (with a black student population of over 75%) wrote the Seattle board, complaining that the " 'boundaries for the Harrison Elementary School were not set in accordance with the long-established standards of the School District . . . but were arbitrarily set with an end to excluding

colored children from McGilvra School, which is adjacent to the Harrison school district.'"

In 1963, at the insistence of the National Association for the Advancement of Colored People (NAACP) and other community groups, the school board adopted a new race-based transfer policy. The new policy added an explicitly racial criterion: If a place exists in a school, then, irrespective of other transfer criteria, a white student may transfer to a predominantly black school, and a black student may transfer to a predominantly white school.

At that time one high school, Garfield, was about two-thirds minority; eight high schools were virtually all white. In 1963, the transfer program's first year, 239 black students and 8 white students transferred. In 1969, about 2,200 (of 10,383 total) of the district's black students and about 400 of the district's white students took advantage of the plan. For the next decade, annual program transfers remained at approximately this level.

3. *The NAACP's First Legal Challenge and Seattle's Response, 1969 to 1977.* In 1969 the NAACP filed a federal lawsuit against the school board, claiming that the board had "unlawfully and unconstitutionally" "establish[ed]" and "maintain[ed]" a system of "racially segregated public schools." The complaint said that 77% of black public elementary school students in Seattle attended 9 of the city's 86 elementary schools and that 23 of the remaining schools had no black students at all. Similarly, of the 1,461 black students enrolled in the 12 senior high schools in Seattle, 1,151 (or 78.8%) attended 3 senior high schools, and 900 (61.6%) attended a single school, Garfield.

The complaint charged that the school board had brought about this segregated system in part by "mak[ing] and enforc[ing]" certain "rules and regulations," in part by "drawing . . . boundary lines" and "executing school attendance policies" that would create and maintain "predominantly Negro or non-white schools," and in part by building schools "in such a manner as to restrict the Negro plaintiffs and the class they represent to predominantly negro or non-white schools." The complaint also charged that the board discriminated in assigning teachers.

The board responded to the lawsuit by introducing a plan that required race-based transfers and mandatory busing. The plan created three new middle schools at three school buildings in the predominantly white north end. It then created a "mixed" student body by assigning to those schools students who would otherwise attend predominantly white, or predominantly black, schools elsewhere. It used explicitly racial criteria in making these assignments (*i.e.*, it deliberately assigned to the new middle schools black students, not white students, from the black schools and white students, not black students, from the white schools). And it used busing to transport the students to their new assignments. The plan provoked considerable local opposition. Opponents brought a lawsuit. But eventually a state court found that the mandatory busing was lawful.

In 1976–1977, the plan involved the busing of about 500 middle school students (300 black students and 200 white students). Another 1,200 black students and 400 white students participated in the previously adopted voluntary transfer program. Thus about 2,000 students out of a total district population of about 60,000 students were involved in one or the other transfer program. At that time, about 20% or 12,000 of the district's students were black. And the board continued to describe 26 of its 112 schools as "segregated."

4. *The NAACP's Second Legal Challenge, 1977.* In 1977, the NAACP filed another legal complaint, this time with the federal Department of Health, Education, and Welfare's Office for Civil Rights (OCR). The complaint alleged that the Seattle School Board had created or perpetuated unlawful racial segregation through, *e.g.*, certain school-transfer criteria, a construction program that needlessly built new schools in white areas, district line-drawing criteria, the maintenance of inferior facilities at black schools, the use of explicit racial criteria in the assignment of teachers and other staff, and a general pattern of delay in respect to the implementation of promised desegregation efforts.

The OCR and the school board entered into a formal settlement agreement. The agreement required the board to implement what became known as the "Seattle Plan."

5. *The Seattle Plan: Mandatory Busing, 1978 to 1988.* The board began to implement the Seattle Plan in 1978. This plan labeled "racially imbalanced" any school at which the percentage of black students exceeded by more than 20% the minority population of the school district as a whole. It applied that label to 26 schools, including 4 high schools—Cleveland (72.8% minority), Franklin (76.6% minority), Garfield (78.4% minority), and Rainier Beach (58.9% minority). The plan paired (or "triaded") "imbalanced" black schools with "imbalanced" white schools. It then placed some grades (say, third and fourth grades) at one school building and other grades (say, fifth and sixth grades) at the other school building. And it thereby required, for example, all fourth grade students from the previ-

ously black and previously white schools first to attend together what would now be a "mixed" fourth grade at one of the school buildings and then the next year to attend what would now be a "mixed" fifth grade at the other school building.

At the same time, the plan provided that a previous "black" school would remain about 50% black, while a previous "white" school would remain about two-thirds white. It was consequently necessary to decide with some care *which* students would attend the new "mixed" grade. For this purpose, administrators cataloged the racial makeup of each neighborhood housing block. The school district met its percentage goals by assigning to the new "mixed" school an appropriate number of "black" housing blocks and "white" housing blocks. At the same time, transport from house to school involved extensive busing, with about half of all students attending a school other than the one closest to their home.

The Seattle Plan achieved the school integration that it sought. Just prior to the plan's implementation, for example, 4 of Seattle's 11 high schools were "imbalanced," *i.e.*, almost exclusively "black" or almost exclusively "white." By 1979, only two were out of "balance." By 1980 only Cleveland remained out of "balance" (as the board defined it) and that by a mere two students.

Nonetheless, the Seattle Plan, due to its busing, provoked serious opposition within the State.[9] Thus, Washington state voters enacted an initiative that amended state law to require students to be assigned to the schools closest to their homes.[10] The Seattle School Board challenged the constitutionality of the initiative.[11] This Court then held that the initiative—which would have prevented the Seattle Plan from taking effect—violated the Fourteenth Amendment.[12]

6. *Student Choice, 1988 to 1998.* By 1988, many white families had left the school district, and many Asian families had moved in. The public school population had fallen from about 100,000 to less than 50,000. The racial makeup of the school population amounted to 43% white, 24% black, and 23% Asian or Pacific Islander, with Hispanics and Native Americans making up the rest. The cost of busing, the harm that members of all racial communities feared that the Seattle Plan caused, the desire to attract white families back to the public schools, and the interest in providing greater school choice led the board to abandon busing and to substitute a new student assignment policy that resembles the plan now before us.

The new plan permitted each student to choose the school he or she wished to attend, subject to race-based constraints. In respect to high schools, for example, a student was given a list of a subset of schools, carefully selected by the board to balance racial distribution in the district by including neighborhood schools and schools in racially different neighborhoods elsewhere in the city. The student could then choose among those schools, indicating a first choice, and other choices the student found acceptable. In making an assignment to a particular high school, the district would give first preference to a student with a sibling already at the school. It gave second preference to a student whose race differed from a race that was "over-represented" at the school (*i.e.,* a race that accounted for a higher percentage of the school population than of the total district population). It gave third preference to students residing in the neighborhood. It gave fourth preference to students who received child care in the neighborhood. In a typical year, say, 1995, about 20,000 potential high school students participated. About 68% received their first choice. Another 16% received an "acceptable" choice. A further 16% were assigned to a school they had not listed.

7. *The Current Plan, 1999 to the Present.* In 1996, the school board adopted the present plan, which began in 1999. In doing so, it sought to deemphasize the use of racial criteria and to increase the likelihood that a student would receive an assignment at his first or second choice high school. The district retained a racial tiebreaker for oversubscribed schools, which takes effect only if the school's minority or majority enrollment falls outside of a 30% range centered on the minority/majority population ratio within the district. At the same time, all students were free subsequently to transfer from the school at which they were initially placed to a different school of their choice without regard to race. Thus, at worst, a student would have to spend one year at a high school he did not pick as a first or second choice.

The new plan worked roughly as expected for the two school years during which it was in effect (1999–2000 and 2000–2001). In the 2000–2001 school year, for example, with the racial tiebreaker, the entering ninth grade class at Franklin High School had a 60% minority population; without the racial tiebreaker that same class at Franklin would have had an almost 80% minority population. (We consider only the ninth grade since only students entering that class were subject to the tiebreaker, and because the plan was not in place long enough to change the composition of an entire school.) In the year 2005–

2006, by which time the racial tiebreaker had not been used for several years, Franklin's overall minority enrollment had risen to 90%. During the period the tiebreaker applied, it typically affected about 300 students per year. Between 80% and 90% of all students received their first choice assignment; between 89% and 97% received their first or second choice assignment.

Petitioner Parents Involved in Community Schools objected to Seattle's most recent plan under the State and Federal Constitutions. In due course, the Washington Supreme Court, the Federal District Court, and the Court of Appeals for the Ninth Circuit (sitting en banc) rejected the challenge and found Seattle's plan lawful.

B

Louisville

1. Before the Lawsuit, 1954 to 1972. In 1956, two years after *Brown* made clear that Kentucky could no longer require racial segregation by law, the Louisville Board of Education created a geography-based student assignment plan designed to help achieve school integration. At the same time it adopted an open transfer policy under which approximately 3,000 of Louisville's 46,000 students applied for transfer. By 1972, however, the Louisville School District remained highly segregated. Approximately half the district's public school enrollment was black; about half was white. Fourteen of the district's nineteen non-vocational middle and high schools were close to totally black or totally white. Nineteen of the district's forty-six elementary schools were between 80% and 100% black. Twenty-one elementary schools were between roughly 90% and 100% white.

2. *Court-Imposed Guidelines and Busing, 1972 to 1991.* In 1972, civil rights groups and parents, claiming unconstitutional segregation, sued the Louisville Board of Education in federal court. The original litigation eventually became a lawsuit against the Jefferson County School System, which in April 1975 absorbed Louisville's schools and combined them with those of the surrounding suburbs. (For ease of exposition, I shall still use "Louisville" to refer to what is now the combined districts.) After preliminary rulings and an eventual victory for the plaintiffs in the Court of Appeals for the Sixth Circuit, the District Court in July 1975 entered an order requiring desegregation.

The order's requirements reflected a (newly enlarged) school district student population of about 135,000, approximately 20% of whom were black. The order required the school board to create and to maintain schools with student populations that ranged, for elementary schools, between 12% and 40% black, and for secondary schools (with one exception), between 12.5% and 35% black.

The District Court also adopted a complex desegregation plan designed to achieve the order's targets. The plan required redrawing school attendance zones, closing 12 schools, and busing groups of students, selected by race and the first letter of their last names, to schools outside their immediate neighborhoods. The plan's initial busing requirements were extensive, involving the busing of 23,000 students and a transportation fleet that had to "operate from early in the morning until late in the evening." For typical students, the plan meant busing for several years (several more years for typical black students than for typical white students). The following notice, published in a Louisville newspaper in 1976, gives a sense of how the district's race-based busing plan operated in practice:

How to tell when your child will be bused...unless

If child's last name begins with letters:	White child will be bused in grades:	Black child will be bused in grades:
A, B, F, Q	11, 12	2, 3, 5, 6, 7, 8, 9, 10, 11, 12
G, H, L	2, 7	2, 3, 4, 6, 7, 8, 9, 10, 11, 12
C, P, R, X	3, 8	2, 3, 4, 5, 6, 7, 8
M, O, T, U, V, Y	4, 9	2, 3, 4, 5, 9, 10, 11, 12
D, E, N, W, Z	5, 10	2, 4, 5, 6, 7, 8, 9, 10, 11, 12
I, J, K, S	6	3, 4, 5, 6, 7, 8, 9, 10, 11, 12

Exempted students:

✔ Kindergarten students
✔ First graders
✔ Students in special schools, primarily for the emotionally or or physically handicapped
✔ Students attending schools exempted under the plan
✔ Some students with specific handicaps

Source: Louisville Courier-Journal, June 18, 1976

Louisville Courier Journal, June 18, 1976 (reproduced in J. Wilkinson, *From Brown to Bakke: The Supreme Court and School Integration 1954–1978*, p. 176 (1979)).

The District Court monitored implementation of the plan. In 1978, it found that the plan had brought all of Louisville's schools within its " 'guidelines' for racial composition" for "at least a substantial portion of the [previous] three years." It removed the case from its active docket while stating that it expected the board "to continue to implement those portions of the desegregation order which are by their nature of a continuing effect."

By 1984, after several schools had fallen out of compliance with the order's racial percentages due to shifting demographics in the community, the school board revised its desegregation plan. In doing so, the board created a new racial "guideline," namely a "floating range of 10% above and 10% below the countywide average for the different grade levels." The board simultaneously redrew district boundaries so that middle school students could attend the same school for three years and high school students for four years. It added "magnet" programs at two high schools. And it adjusted its alphabet-based system for grouping and busing students. The board estimated that its new plan would lead to annual reassignment (with busing) of about 8,500 black students and about 8,000 white students.

3. *Student Choice and Project Renaissance, 1991 to 1996.* By 1991, the board had concluded that assigning elementary school students to two or more schools during their elementary school years had proved educationally unsound and, if continued, would undermine Kentucky's newly adopted Education Reform Act. It consequently conducted a nearly year-long review of its plan. In doing so, it consulted widely with parents and other members of the local community, using public presentations, public meetings, and various other methods to obtain the public's input. At the conclusion of this review, the board adopted a new plan, called "Project Renaissance," that emphasized student choice.

Project Renaissance again revised the board's racial guidelines. It provided that each elementary school would have a black student population of between 15% and 50%; each middle and high school would have a black population and a white population that fell within a range, the boundaries of which were set at 15% above and 15% below the general student population percentages in the county at that grade level. The plan then drew new geographical school assignment zones designed to satisfy these guidelines; the district could reassign students if particular schools failed to meet the guidelines and was required to do so if a school repeatedly missed these targets.

In respect to elementary schools, the plan first drew a neighborhood line around each elementary school, and it then drew a second line around groups of elementary schools (called "clusters"). It initially assigned each student to his or her neighborhood school, but it permitted each student freely to transfer between elementary schools within each cluster *provided that* the transferring student (a) was black if transferring from a predominantly black school to a predominantly white school, or (b) was white if transferring from a predominantly white school to a predominantly black school. Students could also apply to attend magnet elementary schools or programs.

The plan required each middle school student to be assigned to his or her neighborhood school unless the student applied for, and was accepted by, a magnet middle school. The plan provided for "open" high school enrollment. Every 9th or 10th grader could apply to any high school in the system, and the high school would accept applicants according to set criteria— one of which consisted of the need to attain or remain in compliance with the plan's racial guidelines. Finally, the plan created two new magnet schools, one each at the elementary and middle school levels.

4. The Current Plan: Project Renaissance Modified, 1996 to 2003. In 1995 and 1996, the Louisville School Board, with the help of a special "Planning Team," community meetings, and other official and unofficial study groups, monitored the effects of Project Renaissance and considered proposals for improvement. Consequently, in 1996, the board modified Project Renaissance, thereby creating the present plan.

At the time, the district's public school population was approximately 30% black. The plan consequently redrew the racial "guidelines," setting the boundaries at 15% to 50% black for *all* schools. It again redrew school assignment boundaries. And it expanded the transfer opportunities available to elementary and middle school pupils. The plan forbade transfers, however, if the transfer would lead to a school population outside the guideline range, *i.e.*, if it would create a school where fewer than 15% or more than 50% of the students were black.

The plan also established "Parent Assistance Centers" to help parents and students navigate the school selection and assignment process. It pledged the use of other resources in order to "encourage all schools to achieve an African-American enrollment equivalent to the average district-wide African-American enrollment at the school's respective elementary, middle or high school level." And the plan continued use of magnet schools.

In 1999, several parents brought a lawsuit in federal court attacking the plan's use of racial guidelines at one of the district's magnet schools. They asked the court to dissolve the desegregation order and to hold the use of *magnet* school racial guidelines unconstitutional. The board opposed dissolution, arguing that "the old dual system" had left a "demographic imbalance" that "prevent[ed] dissolution." In 2000, after reviewing the present plan, the District Court dissolved the 1975 order. It wrote that there was "overwhelming evidence of the Board's good faith compliance with the desegregation Decree and its underlying purposes." It added that the Louisville School Board had "treated the ideal of an integrated system as much more than a legal obligation—they consider it a positive, desirable policy and an essential element of any well-rounded public school education."

The Court also found that the magnet programs available at the high school in question were "not available at other high schools" in the school district. It consequently held unconstitutional the use of race-based "targets" to govern admission to *magnet schools.* And it ordered the board not to control access to those scarce programs through the use of racial targets.

5. The Current Lawsuit, 2003 to the Present. Subsequent to the District Court's dissolution of the desegregation order (in 2000) the board simply continued to implement its 1996 plan as modified to reflect the court's magnet school determination. In 2003, the petitioner now before us, Crystal Meredith, brought this lawsuit challenging the plan's unmodified portions, *i.e.,* those portions that dealt with *ordinary,* not magnet, schools. Both the District Court and the Court of Appeals for the Sixth Circuit rejected Meredith's challenge and held the unmodified aspects of the plan constitutional.

C

The histories I have set forth describe the extensive and ongoing efforts of two school districts to bring about greater racial integration of their public schools. In both cases the efforts were in part remedial. Louisville began its integration efforts in earnest when a federal court in 1975 entered a school desegregation order. Seattle undertook its integration efforts in response to the filing of a federal lawsuit and as a result of its settlement of a segregation complaint filed with the federal OCR.

The plans in both Louisville and Seattle grow out of these earlier remedial efforts. Both districts faced problems that reflected initial periods of severe racial segregation, followed by such remedial efforts as busing, followed by evidence of resegregation, followed by a need to end busing and encourage the return of, *e.g.*, suburban students through increased student choice. When formulating the plans under review, both districts drew upon their considerable experience with earlier plans, having revised their policies periodically in light of that experience. Both districts rethought their methods over time and explored a wide range of other means, including non-race-conscious policies. Both districts also considered elaborate studies and consulted widely within their communities.

Both districts sought greater racial integration for educational and democratic, as well as for remedial, reasons. Both sought to achieve these objectives while preserving their commitment to other educational goals, *e.g.*, districtwide commitment to high quality public schools, increased pupil assignment to neighborhood schools, diminished use of busing, greater student choice, reduced risk of white flight, and so forth. Consequently, the present plans expand student choice; they limit the burdens (including busing) that earlier plans had imposed upon students and their families; and they use race-conscious criteria in limited and gradually diminishing ways. In particular, they use race-conscious criteria only to mark the outer bounds of broad population-related ranges.

The histories also make clear the futility of looking simply to whether earlier school segregation was *de jure* or *de facto* in order to draw firm lines separating the constitutionally permissible from the constitutionally forbidden use of "race-conscious" criteria. Justice Thomas suggests that it will be easy to identify *de jure* segregation because "[i]n most cases, there either will or will not have been a state constitutional amendment, state statute, local ordinance, or local administrative policy explicitly requiring separation of the races."[13] But our precedent has recognized that *de jure* discrimination can be present even in the absence of racially explicit laws.[14]

No one here disputes that Louisville's segregation was *de jure*. But what about Seattle's? Was it *de facto? De jure?* A mixture? Opinions differed. Or is it that a prior federal court had not adjudicated the matter? Does that make a difference? Is Seattle free on remand to say that its schools were *de jure* segregated, just as in 1956 a memo for the School Board admitted? The plurality does not seem confident as to the answer.[15]

A court finding of *de jure* segregation cannot be the crucial variable. After all, a number of school districts in the South that the Government or private plaintiffs challenged as segregated *by law* voluntarily desegregated their schools *without a court order*—just as Seattle did.[16]

Moreover, Louisville's history makes clear that a community under a court order to desegregate might submit a race-conscious remedial plan *before* the court dissolved the order, but with every intention of following that plan even *after* dissolution. How could such a plan be lawful the day before dissolution but then become unlawful the very next day? On what legal ground can the majority rest its contrary view?[17]

Are courts really to treat as merely *de facto* segregated those school districts that avoided a federal order by voluntarily complying with *Brown*'s requirements?[18] This Court has previously done just the opposite, permitting a race-conscious remedy without any kind of court decree.[19] Because the Constitution emphatically does not forbid the use of race-conscious measures by districts in the South that voluntarily desegregated their schools, on what basis does the plurality claim that the law forbids Seattle to do the same?[20]

The histories also indicate the complexity of the tasks and the practical difficulties that local school boards face when they seek to achieve greater racial integration. The boards work in communities where demographic patterns change, where they must meet traditional learning goals, where they must attract and retain effective teachers, where they should (and will) take account of parents' views and maintain *their* commitment to public school education, where they must adapt to court intervention, where they must encourage voluntary student and parent action—where they will find that their own good faith, their knowledge, and their understanding of local circumstances are always necessary but often insufficient to solve the problems at hand.

These facts and circumstances help explain why in this context, as to means, the law often leaves legislatures, city councils, school boards, and voters with a broad range of choice, thereby giving "different communities" the opportunity to "try different solutions to common problems and gravitate toward those that prove most successful or seem to them best to suit their individual needs."[21]

With this factual background in mind, I turn to the legal question: Does the United States Constitution prohibit these school boards from using race-conscious criteria in the limited ways at issue here?

II

The Legal Standard

A longstanding and unbroken line of legal authority tells us that the Equal Protection Clause permits local school boards to use race-conscious criteria to achieve positive race-related goals, even when the Constitution does not compel it. Because of its importance, I shall repeat what this Court said about the matter in *Swann*. Chief Justice Burger, on behalf of a unanimous Court in a case of exceptional importance, wrote:

> "School authorities are traditionally charged with broad power to formulate and implement educational policy and might well conclude, for example, that in order to prepare students to live in a pluralistic society each school should have a prescribed ratio of Negro to white students reflecting the proportion for the district as a whole. To do this as an educational policy is within the broad discretionary powers of school authorities."[22]

The statement was not a technical holding in the case. But the Court set forth in *Swann* a basic principle of constitutional law—a principle of law that has found "wide acceptance in the legal culture."[23]

Thus, in *North Carolina Bd. of Ed.* v. *Swann*,[24] this Court, citing *Swann*, restated the point. "[S]chool authorities," the Court said, "have wide discretion in formulating school policy, and . . . as a matter of educational policy school authorities may well conclude that some kind of racial balance in the schools is desirable quite apart from any constitutional requirements."

Then-Justice Rehnquist echoed this view in *Bustop, Inc.* v. *Los Angeles Bd. of Ed.*,[25] making clear that he too believed that *Swann*'s statement reflected settled law: "While I have the gravest doubts that [a state supreme court] was *required* by the United States Constitution to take the [desegregation] action that it has taken in this case, I have very little doubt that it was *permitted* by that Constitution to take such action."

These statements nowhere suggest that this freedom is limited to school districts where court-ordered desegregation measures are also in effect. Indeed, in *McDaniel*, a case decided the same day as *Swann*, a group of parents challenged a race-conscious student assignment plan that the Clarke County School Board had *voluntarily* adopted as a remedy without a court order (though under federal agency pressure—pressure Seattle also encountered). The plan required that each elementary school in the district maintain 20% to 40% enrollment of African-American students, corresponding to the racial composition of the district.[26] This Court upheld the plan,[27] rejecting the parents' argument that "a person may not be included or excluded solely because he is a Negro or because he is white."[28]

Federal authorities had claimed—as the NAACP and the OCR did in Seattle—that Clarke County schools were segregated in law, not just in fact. The plurality's claim that Seattle was "never segregated by law" is simply not accurate.[29] The plurality could validly claim that *no court* ever found that Seattle schools were segregated in law. But that is also true of the Clarke County schools in *McDaniel*. Unless we believe that the Constitution enforces one legal standard for the South and another for the North, this Court should grant Seattle the permission it granted Clarke County, Georgia.[30]

This Court has also held that school districts may be required by federal statute to undertake race-conscious desegregation efforts even when there is no likelihood that *de jure* segregation can be shown. In *Board of Ed. of City School Dist. of New York* v. *Harris*,[31] the Court concluded that a federal statute required school districts receiving certain federal funds to remedy faculty segregation, even though in this Court's view the racial disparities in the affected schools were purely *de facto* and would not have been actionable under the Equal Protection Clause. Not even the dissenters thought the race-conscious remedial program posed a *constitutional* problem.[32]

Lower state and federal courts had considered the matter settled and uncontroversial even before this Court decided *Swann*. Indeed, in 1968, the Illinois Supreme Court rejected an equal protection challenge to a race-conscious state law seeking to undo *de facto* segregation:

"To support [their] claim, the defendants heavily rely on three Federal cases, each of which held, no State law being involved, that a local school board does not have an affirmative constitutional duty to act to alleviate racial imbalance in the schools that it did not cause. However, the question as to whether the constitution requires a local school board, or a State, to act to undo *de facto* school segregation is simply not here concerned. The issue here is whether the constitution permits, rather than prohibits, voluntary State action aimed toward reducing and eventually eliminating *de facto* school segregation.

"State laws or administrative policies, directed toward the reduction and eventual elimination of *de facto* segregation of children in the schools and racial imbalance, have been approved by every high State court which has considered the issue. Similarly, the Federal courts which have considered the issue . . . have recognized that voluntary programs of local school authorities designed to alleviate *de facto* segregation and racial imbalance in the schools are not constitutionally forbidden." *Tometz v. Board of Ed., Waukegan School Dist. No. 6.*[33]

I quote the Illinois Supreme Court at length to illustrate the prevailing legal assumption at the time *Swann* was decided. In this respect, *Swann* was not a sharp or unexpected departure from prior rulings; it reflected a consensus that had already emerged among state and lower federal courts.

If there were doubts before *Swann* was decided, they did not survive this Court's decision. Numerous state and federal courts explicitly relied upon *Swann*'s guidance for decades to follow. For instance, a Texas appeals court in 1986 rejected a Fourteenth Amendment challenge to a voluntary integration plan by explaining:

"[T]he absence of a court order to desegregate does not mean that a school board cannot exceed minimum requirements in order to promote school integration. School authorities are traditionally given broad discretionary powers to formulate and implement educational policy and may properly decide to ensure to their students the value of an integrated school experience."[34]

Similarly, in *Zaslawsky v. Bd. of Ed. of Los Angeles City Unified School Dist.*,[35] the Ninth Circuit rejected a federal constitutional challenge to a school district's use of mandatory faculty transfers to ensure that each school's faculty makeup would fall within 10% of the districtwide racial composition. Like the Texas court, the Ninth Circuit relied upon *Swann* and *North Carolina Bd. of Ed.* to reject the argument that "a race-conscious plan is permissible only when there has been a judicial finding of *de jure* segregation."[36] These decisions illustrate well how lower courts understood and followed *Swann*'s enunciation of the relevant legal principle.

Courts are not alone in accepting as constitutionally valid the legal principle that *Swann* enunciated—*i.e.*, that the government may voluntarily adopt race-conscious measures to improve conditions of race even when it is not under a constitutional obligation to do so. That principle has been accepted by every branch of government and is rooted in the history of the Equal Protection Clause itself. Thus, Congress has enacted numerous race-conscious statutes that illustrate that principle or rely upon its validity.[37] In fact, without being exhaustive, I have counted 51 federal statutes that use racial classifications. I have counted well over 100 state statutes that similarly employ racial classifications. Presidential administrations for the past half-century have used and supported various race-conscious measures.[38] And during the same time, hundreds of local school districts have adopted student assignment plans that use race-conscious criteria.[39]

That *Swann*'s legal statement should find such broad acceptance is not surprising. For *Swann* is predicated upon a well-established legal view of the Fourteenth Amendment. That view understands the basic objective of those who wrote the Equal Protection Clause as forbidding practices that lead to racial exclusion. The Amendment sought to bring into American society as full members those whom the Nation had previously held in slavery.[40]

There is reason to believe that those who drafted an Amendment with this basic purpose in mind would have understood the legal and practical difference between the use of race-conscious criteria in defiance of that purpose, namely to keep the races apart, and the use of race-conscious criteria to further that purpose, namely to bring the races together.[41] Although the Constitution almost always forbids the former, it is significantly more lenient in respect to the latter.[42]

Sometimes Members of this Court have disagreed about the degree of leniency that the Clause affords to programs designed to include.[43] But I can find no case in which this Court has followed Justice Thomas' "colorblind" approach. And I have found no case that otherwise repudiated this constitutional asymmetry between that which seeks to *exclude* and that which seeks to *include* members of minority races.

What does the plurality say in response? First, it seeks to distinguish *Swann* and other similar cases on the ground that those cases involved remedial plans in response to *judicial findings* of *de jure* segregation. As *McDaniel* and *Harris* show, that is historically untrue.[44] Many school districts in the South adopted segregation remedies (to which *Swann* clearly applies) without any such federal order.[45] Seattle's circumstances are not meaningfully different from those in, say, *McDaniel*, where this Court approved race-conscious remedies. Louisville's plan was created and initially adopted when a compulsory district court order was in place. And, in any event, the histories of Seattle and Louisville make clear that this distinction—between court-ordered and voluntary desegregation—seeks a line that sensibly cannot be drawn.

Second, the plurality downplays the importance of *Swann* and related cases by frequently describing their relevant statements as "dicta." These criticisms, however, miss the main point. *Swann* did not hide its understanding of the law in a corner of an obscure opinion or in a footnote, unread but by experts. It set forth its view prominently in an important opinion joined by all nine Justices, knowing that it would be read and followed throughout the Nation. The basic problem with the plurality's technical "dicta"-based response lies in its overly theoretical approach to case law, an approach that emphasizes rigid distinctions between holdings and dicta in a way that serves to mask the radical nature of today's decision. Law is not an exercise in mathematical logic. And statements of a legal rule set forth in a judicial opinion do not always divide neatly into "holdings" and "dicta." (Consider the legal "status" of Justice Powell's separate opinion in *Regents of Univ. of Cal. v. Bakke.*[46]) The constitutional principle enunciated in *Swann*, reiterated in subsequent cases, and relied upon over many years, provides, and has widely been thought to provide, authoritative legal guidance. And if the plurality now chooses to reject that principle, it cannot adequately justify its retreat simply by affixing the label "dicta" to reasoning with which it disagrees. Rather, it must explain to the courts and to the Nation *why* it would abandon guidance set forth many years before, guidance that countless others have built upon over time, and which the law has continuously embodied.

Third, a more important response is the plurality's claim that later cases—in particular *Johnson, Adarand*, and *Grutter*—supplanted *Swann.*[47] The plurality says that cases such as *Swann* and the others I have described all "were decided before this Court definitively determined that 'all racial classifications . . . must be analyzed by a reviewing court under strict scrutiny.'"[48] This Court in *Adarand* added that "such classifications are constitutional only if they are narrowly tailored measures that further compelling governmental interests."[49] And the Court repeated this same statement in *Grutter*.[50]

Several of these cases were significantly more restrictive than *Swann* in respect to the degree of leniency the Fourteenth Amendment grants to programs designed to *include* people of all races.[51] But that legal circumstance cannot make a critical difference here for two separate reasons.

First, no case—not *Adarand*, *Gratz*, *Grutter*, or any other—has ever held that the test of "strict scrutiny" means that all racial classifications—no matter whether they seek to include or exclude—must in practice be treated the same. The Court did not say in *Adarand* or in *Johnson* or in *Grutter* that it was overturning *Swann* or its central constitutional principle.

Indeed, in its more recent opinions, the Court recognized that the "fundamental purpose" of strict scrutiny review is to "take relevant differences" between "fundamentally different situations . . . into account."[52] The Court made clear that "[s]trict scrutiny does not trea[t] dissimilar race-based decisions as though they were equally objectionable." *Ibid*. It added that the fact that a law "treats [a person] unequally because of his or her race . . . says nothing about the ultimate validity of any particular law."[53] And the Court, using the very phrase that Justice Marshall had used to describe strict scrutiny's application to any *exclusionary* use of racial criteria, sought to "*dispel the notion* that strict scrutiny" is as likely to condemn *inclusive* uses of "race-conscious" criteria as it is to invalidate *exclusionary* uses. That is, it is *not* in all circumstances " 'strict in theory, but fatal in fact.' "[54]

The Court in *Grutter* elaborated:

"Strict scrutiny is not 'strict in theory, but fatal in fact.' . . . Although all governmental uses of race are subject to strict scrutiny, not all are invalidated by it. . . .

"Context matters when reviewing race-based governmental action under the Equal Protection Clause.[55] . . . Not every decision influenced by race is equally objectionable, and strict scrutiny is designed to provide a framework for carefully examining the importance and the sincerity of the reasons advanced by the governmental decisionmaker for the use of race in that particular context."[56]

The Court's holding in *Grutter* demonstrates that the Court meant what it said, for the Court upheld an elite law school's race-conscious admissions program.

The upshot is that the cases to which the plurality refers, though all applying strict scrutiny, do not treat exclusive and inclusive uses the same. Rather, they apply the strict scrutiny test in a manner that is "fatal in fact" only to racial classifications that harmfully *exclude;* they apply the test in a manner that is *not* fatal in fact to racial classifications that seek to *include.*

The plurality cannot avoid this simple fact.[57] Today's opinion reveals that the plurality would rewrite this Court's prior jurisprudence, at least in practical application, transforming the "strict scrutiny" test into a rule that is fatal in fact across the board. In doing so, the plurality parts company from this Court's prior cases, and it takes from local government the longstanding legal right to use race-conscious criteria for inclusive purposes in limited ways.

Second, as *Grutter* specified, "[c]ontext matters when reviewing race-based governmental action under the Equal Protection Clause."[58] And contexts differ dramatically one from the other. Governmental use of race-based criteria can arise in the context of, for example, census forms, research expenditures for diseases, assignments of police officers patrolling predominantly minority-race neighborhoods, efforts to desegregate racially segregated schools, policies that favor minorities when distributing goods or services in short supply, actions that create majority-minority electoral districts, peremptory strikes that remove potential jurors on the basis of race, and others. Given the significant differences among these contexts, it would be surprising if the law required an identically strict legal test for evaluating the constitutionality of race-based criteria as to each of them.

Here, the context is one in which school districts seek to advance or to maintain racial integration in primary and secondary schools. It is a context, as *Swann* makes clear, where history has required special administrative remedies. And it is a context in which the school boards' plans simply set race-conscious limits at the outer boundaries of a broad range.

This context is *not* a context that involves the use of race to decide who will receive goods or services that are normally distributed on the basis of merit and which are in short supply. It is not one in which race-conscious limits stigmatize or exclude; the limits at issue do not pit the races against each other or otherwise significantly exacerbate racial tensions. They do not impose burdens unfairly upon members of one race alone but instead seek benefits for members of all races alike. The context here is one of racial limits that seek, not to keep the races apart, but to bring them together.

The importance of these differences is clear once one compares the present circumstances with other cases where one or more of these negative features are present.[59]

If one examines the context more specifically, one finds that the districts' plans reflect efforts to overcome a history of segregation, embody the results of broad experience and community consultation, seek to expand student choice while reducing the need for mandatory busing, and use race-conscious criteria in highly limited ways that diminish the use of race compared to preceding integration efforts.[60] They do not seek to award a scarce commodity on the basis of merit, for they are not magnet schools; rather, by design and in practice, they offer substantially equivalent academic programs and electives. Although some parents or children prefer some schools over others, school popularity has varied significantly over the years. In 2000, for example, Roosevelt was the most popular first choice high school in Seattle; in 2001, Ballard was the most popular; in 2000, West Seattle was one of the least popular; by 2003, it was one of the more popular.[61] In a word, the school plans under review do not involve the kind of race-based harm that has led this Court, in other contexts, to find the use of race-conscious criteria unconstitutional.

These and related considerations convinced one Ninth Circuit judge in the Seattle case to apply a standard of constitutionality review that is less than "strict," and to conclude that this Court's precedents do not require the contrary.[62]

The view that a more lenient standard than "strict scrutiny" should apply in the present context would not imply abandonment of judicial efforts carefully to determine the need for race-conscious criteria and the criteria's tailoring in light of the need.

And the present context requires a court to examine carefully the race-conscious program at issue. In doing so, a reviewing judge must be fully aware of the potential dangers and pitfalls that Justice Thomas and Justice Kennedy mention.[63]

But unlike the plurality, such a judge would also be aware that a legislature or school administrators, ultimately accountable to the electorate, could *nonetheless* properly conclude that a racial classification sometimes serves a purpose important enough to overcome the risks they mention, for example, helping to end racial isolation or to achieve a diverse student body in public schools.[64] Where that is so, the judge would carefully examine the program's details to determine whether the use of race-conscious criteria is proportionate to the important ends it serves.

In my view, this contextual approach to scrutiny is altogether fitting. I believe that the law requires application here of a standard of review that is not "strict" in the traditional sense of that word, although it does require the careful review I have just described.[65] Apparently Justice Kennedy also agrees that strict scrutiny would not apply in respect to certain "race-conscious" school board policies. See *ante*, at 9 ("Executive and legislative branches, which for generations now have considered these types of policies and procedures, should be permitted to employ them with candor and with confidence that a constitutional violation does not occur whenever a decisionmaker considers the impact a given approach might have on students of different races").

Nonetheless, in light of *Grutter* and other precedents,[66] I shall adopt the first alternative. I shall apply the version of strict scrutiny that those cases embody. I shall consequently ask whether the school boards in Seattle and Louisville adopted these plans to serve a "compelling governmental interest" and, if so, whether the plans are "narrowly tailored" to achieve that interest. If the plans survive this strict review, they would survive less exacting review *a fortiori*. Hence, I conclude that the plans before us pass both parts of the strict scrutiny test. Consequently I must conclude that the plans here are permitted under the Constitution.

III

Applying the Legal Standard

A
Compelling Interest

The principal interest advanced in these cases to justify the use of race-based criteria goes by various names. Sometimes a court refers to it as an interest in achieving racial "diversity." Other times a court, like the plurality here, refers to it as an interest in racial "balancing." I have used more general terms to signify that interest, describing it, for example, as an interest in promoting or preserving greater racial "integration" of public schools. By this term, I mean the school districts' interest in eliminating school-by-school racial isolation and increasing the degree to which racial mixture characterizes each of the district's schools and each individual student's public school experience.

Regardless of its name, however, the interest at stake possesses three essential elements. First, there is a historical and remedial element: an interest in setting right the consequences of prior conditions of segregation. This refers back to a time when public schools were highly segregated, often as a result of legal or administrative policies that facilitated racial segregation in public schools. It is an interest in continuing to combat the remnants of segregation caused in whole or in part by these school-related policies, which have often affected not only schools, but also housing patterns, employment practices, economic conditions, and social attitudes. It is an interest in maintaining hard-won gains. And it has its roots in preventing what gradually may become the de facto resegregation of America's public schools.[67]

Second, there is an educational element: an interest in overcoming the adverse educational effects produced by and associated with highly segregated schools.[68] Studies suggest that children taken from those schools and placed in integrated settings often show positive academic gains.[69]

Other studies reach different conclusions.[70] But the evidence supporting an educational interest in racially integrated schools is well established and strong enough to permit a democratically elected school board reasonably to determine that this interest is a compelling one.

Research suggests, for example, that black children from segregated educational environments significantly increase their achievement levels once they are placed in a more integrated setting. Indeed in Louisville itself the achievement gap between black and white elementary school students grew substantially smaller (by seven percentage points) after the integration plan was implemented in 1975.[71] Conversely, to take another example, evidence from a district in Norfolk, Virginia, shows that re-segregated schools led to a decline in the achievement test scores of children of all races.[72]

One commentator, reviewing dozens of studies of the educational benefits of desegregated schooling, found that the studies have provided "remarkably consistent" results, showing that: (1) black students' educational achievement is improved in integrated schools as compared to racially isolated schools, (2) black students' educational achievement is improved in integrated classes, and (3) the earlier that black students are removed from racial isolation, the better their educational outcomes.[73] Multiple studies also indicate that black alumni of integrated schools are more likely to move into occupations traditionally closed to African-Americans, and to earn more money in those fields.[74]

Third, there is a democratic element: an interest in producing an educational environment that reflects the "pluralistic society" in which our children will live.[75] It is an interest in helping our children learn to work and play together with children of different racial backgrounds. It is an interest in teaching children to engage in the kind of cooperation among Americans of all races that is necessary to make a land of three hundred million people one Nation.

Again, data support this insight.[76]

There are again studies that offer contrary conclusions.[77] Again, however, the evidence supporting a democratic interest in racially integrated schools is firmly established and sufficiently strong to permit a school board to determine, as this Court has itself often found, that this interest is compelling.

For example, one study documented that "black and white students in desegregated schools are less racially prejudiced than those in segregated schools," and that "interracial contact in desegregated schools leads to an increase in interracial sociability and friendship."[78] Other studies have found that both black and white students who attend integrated schools are more likely to work in desegregated companies after graduation than students who attended racially isolated schools.[79] Further research has shown that the desegregation of schools can help bring adult communities together by reducing segregated housing. Cities that have implemented successful school desegregation plans have witnessed increased interracial contact and neighborhoods that tend to become less racially segregated.[80] These effects not only reinforce the prior gains of integrated primary and secondary education; they also foresee a time when there is less need to use race-conscious criteria.

Moreover, this Court from *Swann* to *Grutter* has treated these civic effects as an important virtue of racially diverse education.[81] In *Grutter*, in the context of law school admissions, we found that these types of interests were, constitutionally speaking, "compelling."[82]

In light of this Court's conclusions in *Grutter,* the "compelling" nature of these interests in the context of primary and secondary public education follows here *a fortiori*. Primary and secondary schools are where the education of this Nation's children begins, where each of us begins to absorb those values we carry with us to the end of our days. As Justice Marshall said, "unless our children begin to learn together, there is little hope that our people will ever learn to live together."[83]

And it was *Brown*, after all, focusing upon primary and secondary schools, not *Sweatt* v. *Painter*,[84] focusing on law schools, or *McLaurin* v. *Oklahoma State Regents for Higher Ed.*,[85] focusing on graduate schools, that affected so deeply not only Americans but the world.[86] Hence, I am not surprised that Justice Kennedy finds that, "a district may consider it a compelling interest to achieve a diverse student population," including a *racially* diverse population.[87]

The compelling interest at issue here, then, includes an effort to eradicate the remnants, not of general "societal discrimination,"[88] but of primary and secondary school segregation[89]; it includes an effort to create school environments that provide better educational opportunities for all children; it includes an effort to help create citizens better prepared to know, to understand, and to work with people of all races and backgrounds, thereby furthering the kind of democratic government our Constitution foresees. If an educational interest that combines these three elements is not "compelling," what is?

The majority acknowledges that in prior cases this Court has recognized at least two interests as compelling: an interest in "remedying the effects of past intentional discrimination," and an interest in "diversity in higher education."[90] But the plurality does not convincingly explain why those interests do not constitute a "compelling interest" here. How do the remedial interests here differ in kind from those at issue in the voluntary desegregation efforts that Attorney General Kennedy many years ago described in his letter to the President?[91] How do the educational and civic interests differ in kind from those that underlie and justify the racial "diversity" that the law school sought in *Grutter*, where this Court found a compelling interest?

The plurality tries to draw a distinction by reference to the well-established conceptual difference between *de jure* segregation ("segregation by state action") and *de facto* segregation ("racial imbalance caused by other factors").[92] But that distinction concerns what the Constitution *requires* school boards to do, not what it *permits* them to do.[93]

The opinions cited by the plurality to justify its reliance upon the *de jure/de facto* distinction only address what remedial measures a school district may be constitutionally *required* to undertake.[94] As to what is *permitted*, nothing in our equal protection law suggests that a State may right only those wrongs that it committed. No case of this Court has ever relied upon the *de jure/de facto* distinction in order to limit what a school district is voluntarily allowed to do. That is what is at issue here. And *Swann, McDaniel, Crawford, North Carolina Bd. of Ed., Harris,* and *Bustop* made one thing clear: significant as the difference between *de jure* and *de facto* segregation may be to the question of what a school district *must* do, that distinction is not germane to the question of what a school district *may* do.

Nor does any precedent indicate, as the plurality suggests with respect to Louisville,[95] that remedial interests vanish the day after a federal court declares that a district is "unitary." Of course, Louisville adopted those portions of the plan at issue here *before* a court declared Louisville "unitary." Moreover, in *Freeman*, this Court pointed out that in "one sense of the term, vestiges of past segregation by state decree do remain in our society and in our schools. Past wrongs to the black race, wrongs committed by the State and in its name, are a stubborn fact of history. And stubborn facts of history linger and persist."[96] I do not understand why this Court's cases, which rest the significance of a "unitary" finding in part upon the wisdom and desirability of returning schools to local control, should deprive those local officials of legal *permission* to use means they once found necessary to combat persisting injustices.

For his part, Justice Thomas faults my citation of various studies supporting the view that school districts can find compelling educational and civic interests in integrating their public schools.[97] He is entitled of course to his own opinion as to which studies he finds convincing—although it bears mention that even the author of some of Justice Thomas' preferred studies has found *some* evidence linking integrated learning environments to increased academic achievement.[98] If we are to insist upon unanimity in the social science literature before finding a compelling interest, we might never find one. I believe only that the Constitution allows democratically elected school boards to make up their own minds as to how best to include people of all races in one America.

B

Narrow Tailoring

I next ask whether the plans before us are "narrowly tailored" to achieve these "compelling" objectives. I shall not accept the school board's assurances on faith,[99] and I shall subject the "tailoring" of their plans to "rigorous judicial review."[100] Several factors, taken together, nonetheless lead me to conclude that the boards' use of race-conscious criteria in these plans passes even the strictest "tailoring" test.

First, the race-conscious criteria at issue only help set the outer bounds of *broad* ranges.[101] They constitute but one part of plans that depend primarily upon other, nonracial elements. To use race in this way is not to set a forbidden "quota."[102]

In fact, the defining feature of both plans is greater emphasis upon student choice. In Seattle, for example, in more than 80% of all cases, that choice alone determines which high schools Seattle's ninth graders will attend. After ninth grade, students can decide voluntarily to transfer to a preferred district high school (without any consideration of race-conscious criteria). *Choice,* therefore, is the "predominant factor" in these plans. *Race* is not.[103]

Indeed, the race-conscious ranges at issue in these cases often have no effect, either because the particular school is not oversubscribed in the year in question, or because the racial makeup of the school falls within the broad range, or because the student is a transfer applicant or has a sibling at the school. In these respects, the broad ranges are less like a quota and more like the kinds of "useful starting points" that this Court has consistently found permissible, even when they set boundaries upon voluntary transfers, and even when they are based upon a community's general population.[104]

Second, broad-range limits on voluntary school choice plans are less burdensome, and hence more narrowly tailored,[105] than other race-conscious restrictions this Court has previously approved.[106] Indeed, the plans before us are *more narrowly tailored* than the race-conscious admission plans that this Court approved in *Grutter.* Here, race becomes a factor only in a fraction of students' non-merit-based assignments—not in large numbers of students' merit-based applications. Moreover, the effect of applying race-conscious criteria here affects potentially disadvantaged students *less severely,* not more severely, than the criteria at issue in *Grutter.* Disappointed students are not rejected from a State's flagship graduate program; they simply attend a different one of the district's many public schools, which in aspiration and in fact are substantially equal.[107] And, in Seattle, the disadvantaged student loses at most one year at the high school of his choice. One will search *Grutter* in vain for similarly persuasive evidence of narrow tailoring as the school districts have presented here.

Third, the manner in which the school boards developed these plans itself reflects "narrow tailoring." Each plan was devised to overcome a history of segregated public schools. Each plan embodies the results of local experience and community consultation. Each plan is the product of a process that has sought to enhance student choice, while diminishing the need for mandatory busing. And each plan's use of race-conscious elements is *diminished* compared to the use of race in preceding integration plans.

The school boards' widespread consultation, their experimentation with numerous other plans, indeed, the 40-year history that Part I sets forth, make clear that plans that are less explicitly race-based are unlikely to achieve the board's "compelling" objectives. The history of each school system reveals highly segregated schools, followed by remedial plans that involved forced busing, followed by efforts to attract or retain students through the use of plans that abandoned busing and replaced it with greater student choice. Both cities once tried to achieve more integrated schools by relying solely upon measures such as redrawn district boundaries, new school building construction, and unrestricted voluntary transfers. In neither city did these prior attempts prove sufficient to achieve the city's integration goals.[108]

Moreover, giving some degree of weight to a local school board's knowledge, expertise, and concerns in these particular matters is not inconsistent with rigorous judicial scrutiny. It simply recognizes that judges are not well suited to act as school administrators. Indeed, in the context of school desegregation, this Court has repeatedly stressed the importance of acknowledging that local school boards better understand their own communities and have a better knowledge of what in practice will best meet the educational needs of their pupils.[109]

Experience in Seattle and Louisville is consistent with experience elsewhere. In 1987, the U.S. Commission on Civil Rights studied 125 large school districts seeking integration. It reported that most districts—92 of them, in fact—adopted desegregation policies that combined two or more highly race-conscious strategies, for example, rezoning or pairing.[110]

Having looked at dozens of *amicus* briefs, public reports, news stories, and the records in many of this Court's prior cases, which together span 50 years of desegregation history in school districts across the Nation, I have discovered many examples of districts that sought integration through explicitly race-conscious methods, including mandatory busing. Yet, I have found *no* example or model that would permit this Court to say to Seattle and to Louisville: "Here is an instance of a desegregation plan that is likely to achieve your objectives and also makes less use of race-conscious criteria than your plans." And, if the plurality cannot suggest such a model—and it cannot—then it seeks to impose a "narrow tailoring" requirement that in practice would never be met.

Indeed, if there is no such plan, or if such plans are purely imagined, it is understandable why, as the plurality notes,[111] Seattle school officials concentrated on diminishing the racial component of their districts' plan, but did not pursue eliminating that element entirely. For the plurality now to insist as it does,[112] that these school districts ought to have said so officially is either to ask for the superfluous (if they need only make explicit what is implicit) or to demand the impossible (if they must somehow provide more proof that there is no hypothetical *other* plan that could work as well as theirs). I am not aware of any case in which this Court has read the "narrow tailoring" test to impose such a requirement.[113]

The plurality also points to the school districts' use of numerical goals based upon the racial breakdown of the general school population, and it faults the districts for failing to prove that *no other set of numbers will work.*[114] The plurality refers to no case in support of its demand. Nor is it likely to find such a case. After all, this Court has in many cases explicitly permitted districts to use target ratios based upon the district's underlying population.[115] The reason is obvious: In Seattle, where the overall student population is 41% white, permitting 85% white enrollment at a single school would make it much more likely that other schools would have very few white students, whereas in Jefferson County, with a 60% white enrollment, one school with 85% white students would be less likely to skew enrollments elsewhere.

Moreover, there is research-based evidence supporting, for example, that a ratio no greater than 50% minority—which is Louisville's starting point, and as close as feasible to Seattle's starting point—is helpful in limiting the risk of "white flight."[116] Federal law also assumes that a similar target percentage will help avoid detrimental "minority group isolation."[117] What other numbers are the boards to use as a "starting point"? Are they to spend days, weeks, or months seeking independently to validate the use of ratios that this Court has repeatedly authorized in prior cases? Are they to draw numbers out of thin air? These districts have followed this Court's holdings and advice in "tailoring" their plans. That, too, strongly supports the lawfulness of their methods.

Nor could the school districts have accomplished their desired aims (*e.g.*, avoiding forced busing, countering white flight, maintaining racial diversity) by other means. Nothing in the extensive history of desegregation efforts over the past 50 years gives the districts, or this Court, any reason to believe that another method is possible to accomplish these goals. Nevertheless, Justice Kennedy suggests that school boards:

> "may pursue the goal of bringing together students of diverse backgrounds and races through other means, including strategic site selection of new schools; drawing attendance zones with general recognition of the demographics of neighborhoods; allocating resources for special programs; recruiting students and faculty in a targeted fashion; and tracking enrollments, performance, and other statistics by race."[118]

But, as to "strategic site selection," Seattle has built one new high school in the last 44 years (and that specialized school serves only 300 students). In fact, six of the Seattle high schools involved in this case were built by the 1920s; the other four were open by the early 1960s.[119] As to "drawing" neighborhood "attendance zones" on a racial basis, Louisville tried it, and it worked only when forced busing was also part of the plan.[120] As to "allocating resources for special programs," Seattle and Louisville have both experimented with this; indeed, these programs are often referred to as "magnet schools," but the limited desegregation effect of these efforts extends at most to those few schools to which additional resources are granted. In addition, there is no evidence from the experience of these school districts that it will make any meaningful impact.[121] As to "recruiting faculty" on the basis of race, both cities have tried, but only as one part of a broader program. As to "tracking enrollments, performance and other statistics by race," tracking *reveals* the problem; it does not cure it.

Justice Kennedy sets forth two additional concerns related to "narrow tailoring." In respect to Louisville, he says first that officials stated (1) that kindergarten assignments are not subject to the race-conscious guidelines, and (2) that the child at issue here was denied permission to attend the kindergarten he wanted because of those guidelines. Both, he explains, cannot be true. He adds that this confusion illustrates that Louisville's assignment plan (or its explanation of it to this Court) is insufficiently precise in respect to "who makes the decisions," "oversight," "the precise circumstances in which an assignment decision" will be made; and "which of two similarly situated children will be subjected to a given race-based decision."[122]

The record suggests, however, that the child in question was not assigned to the school he preferred because he missed the kindergarten application deadline.[123] After he had enrolled and after the academic year had begun, he then applied to transfer to his preferred school after the kindergarten assignment deadline had passed,[124] possibly causing school officials to treat his late request as an application to transfer to the first grade, in respect to which the guidelines apply. I am not certain just how the remainder of Justice Kennedy's concerns affect the lawfulness of the Louisville program, for they seem to be failures of explanation, not of administration. But Louisville should be able to answer the relevant questions on remand.

Justice Kennedy's second concern is directly related to the

merits of Seattle's plan: Why does Seattle's plan group Asian-Americans, Hispanic-Americans, Native-Americans, and African-Americans together, treating all as similar minorities?[125] The majority suggests that Seattle's classification system could permit a school to be labeled "diverse" with a 50% Asian-American and 50% white student body, and no African-American students, Hispanic students, or students of other ethnicity.[126]

The 50/50 hypothetical has no support in the record here; it is conjured from the imagination. In fact, Seattle apparently began to treat these different minority groups alike in response to the federal Emergency School Aid Act's requirement that it do so.[127] Moreover, maintaining this federally mandated system of classification makes sense insofar as Seattle's experience indicates that the relevant circumstances in respect to each of these different minority groups are roughly similar, *e.g.*, in terms of residential patterns, and call for roughly similar responses. This is confirmed by the fact that Seattle has been able to achieve a desirable degree of diversity without the *greater* emphasis on race that drawing fine lines among minority groups would require. Does the plurality's view of the Equal Protection Clause mean that courts must give no weight to such a board determination? Does it insist upon especially strong evidence supporting inclusion of multiple minority groups in an otherwise lawful government minority-assistance program? If so, its interpretation threatens to produce divisiveness among minority groups that is incompatible with the basic objectives of the Fourteenth Amendment. Regardless, the plurality cannot object that the constitutional defect is the individualized use of race and simultaneously object that not enough account of individuals' race has been taken.

Finally, I recognize that the Court seeks to distinguish *Grutter* from these cases by claiming that *Grutter* arose in " 'the context of higher education.' "[128] But that is not a meaningful legal distinction. I have explained why I do not believe the Constitution could possibly find "compelling" the provision of a racially diverse education for a 23-year-old law student but not for a 13-year-old high school pupil.[129] And I have explained how the plans before us are more narrowly tailored than those in *Grutter.*[130] I add that one cannot find a relevant distinction in the fact that these school districts did not examine the merits of applications "individual[ly]."[131] The context here does not involve admission by merit; a child's academic, artistic, and athletic "merits" are not at all relevant to the child's placement. These are not affirmative action plans, and hence "individualized scrutiny" is simply beside the point.

The upshot is that these plans' specific features—(1) their limited and historically-diminishing use of race, (2) their strong reliance upon other non-race-conscious elements, (3) their history and the manner in which the districts developed and modified their approach, (4) the comparison with prior plans, and (5) the lack of reasonably evident alternatives—together show that the districts' plans are "narrowly tailored" to achieve their "compelling" goals. In sum, the districts' race-conscious plans satisfy "strict scrutiny" and are therefore lawful.

IV

Direct Precedent

Two additional precedents more directly related to the plans here at issue reinforce my conclusion. The first consists of the District Court determination in the Louisville case when it dissolved its desegregation order that there was "overwhelming evidence of the Board's good faith compliance with the desegregation Decree and its underlying purposes," indeed that the Board had "treated the ideal of an integrated system as much more than a legal obligation—they consider it a positive, desirable policy and an essential element of any well-rounded public school education."[132] When the court made this determination in 2000, it did so in the context of the Louisville desegregation plan that the board had adopted in 1996. That plan, which took effect before 1996, is the very plan that in all relevant respects is in effect now and is the subject of the present challenge.

No one claims that (the relevant portion of) Louisville's plan was unlawful in 1996 when Louisville adopted it. To the contrary, there is every reason to believe that it represented part of an effort to implement the 1978 desegregation order. But if the plan was lawful when it was first adopted and if it was lawful the day before the District Court dissolved its order, how can the plurality now suggest that it became *unlawful* the following day? Is it conceivable that the Constitution, implemented through a court desegregation order, could permit (perhaps *require*) the district to make use of a race-conscious plan the day before the order was dissolved and then *forbid* the district to use the identical plan the day after?[133] The Equal Protection Clause is not incoherent. And federal courts would rightly hesitate to find unitary status if the consequences of the ruling were so dramatically disruptive.

Second, *Seattle School Dist. No. 1*,[134] is directly on point. That case involves the original Seattle Plan, a *more heavily race-conscious predecessor* of the very plan now before us. In *Seattle School Dist. No. 1*, this Court struck down a state referendum that effectively barred implementation of Seattle's desegregation plan and "burden[ed] all future attempts to integrate Washington schools in districts throughout the State."[135] Because the referendum would have prohibited the adoption of a school-integration plan that involved mandatory busing, and because it would have imposed a special burden on school integration plans (plans that sought to integrate previously segregated schools), the Court found it unconstitutional.[136]

In reaching this conclusion, the Court did not directly address the constitutional merits of the underlying Seattle plan. But it explicitly cited *Swann*'s statement that the Constitution permitted a local district to adopt such a plan.[137] It also cited to Justice Powell's opinion in *Bakke, approving of* the limited use of race-conscious criteria in a university-admissions "affirmative action" case.[138] In addition, the Court stated that "[a]ttending an ethnically diverse school,"[139] could help prepare "minority children for citizenship in our pluralistic society," hopefully "teaching members of the racial majority to live in harmony and mutual respect with children of minority heritage."[140]

It is difficult to believe that the Court that held unconstitutional a referendum that would have interfered with the implementation of this plan thought that the integration plan it sought to preserve was itself an *unconstitutional* plan. And if

Seattle School Dist. No. 1 is premised upon the constitutional-ity of the original Seattle Plan, it is equally premised upon the constitutionality of the present plan, for the present plan *is* the Seattle Plan, modified only insofar as it places even *less* empha-sis on race-conscious elements than its predecessors.

It is even more difficult to accept the plurality's contrary view, namely that the underlying plan was unconstitutional. If that is so, then *all* of Seattle's earlier (even more race-conscious) plans must also have been unconstitutional. That necessary implication of the plurality's position strikes the 13th chime of the clock. How could the plurality adopt a constitutional stan-dard that would hold unconstitutional large numbers of race-conscious integration plans adopted by numerous school boards over the past 50 years while remaining true to this Court's de-segregation precedent?

V

Consequences

The Founders meant the Constitution as a practical docu-ment that would transmit its basic values to future generations through principles that remained workable over time. Hence it is important to consider the potential consequences of the plu-rality's approach, as measured against the Constitution's objec-tives. To do so provides further reason to believe that the plural-ity's approach is legally unsound.

For one thing, consider the effect of the plurality's views on the parties before us and on similar school districts throughout the Nation. Will Louisville and all similar school districts have to return to systems like Louisville's initial 1956 plan, which did not consider race at all?[141] That initial 1956 plan proved ineffective. Sixteen years into the plan, 14 of 19 middle and high schools remained almost totally white or almost totally black.[142]

The districts' past and current plans are not unique. They resemble other plans, promulgated by hundreds of local school boards, which have attempted a variety of desegregation methods that have evolved over time in light of experience. A 1987 Civil Rights Commission Study of 125 school districts in the Nation demonstrated the breadth and variety of desegregation plans:

"The [study] documents almost 300 desegregation plans that were implemented between 1961 and 1985. The degree of heterogeneity within these districts is immediately apparent. They are located in every region of the country and range in size from Las Cruces, New Mexico, with barely over 15,000 students attending 23 schools in 1968, to New York City, with more than one million students in 853 schools. The sample includes districts in urban areas of all sizes, suburbs (*e.g.*, Arlington County, Virginia) and rural areas (*e.g.*, Jefferson Parish, Louisiana, and Raleigh County, West Virginia). It contains 34 countywide districts with central cities (the 11 Florida districts fit this description, plus Clark County, Nevada and others) and a small number of consolidated districts (New Castle County, Delaware and Jefferson County, Kentucky).

"The districts also vary in their racial compositions and levels of segregation. Initial plans were implemented in Mobile, Alabama and Mecklenburg County, North Carolina, and in a number of other southern districts in the face of total racial segregation. At the other extreme, Santa Clara, California had a relatively even racial distribution prior to its 1979 desegregation plan. When the 1965 plan was designed for Harford County, Maryland, the district was 92 percent white. Compton, California, on the other hand, became over 99 percent black in the 1980s, while Buffalo, New York had a virtual 50–50 split between white and minority students prior to its 1977 plan.

"It is not surprising to find a large number of different desegregation strategies in a sample with this much variation."[143]

A majority of these desegregation techniques explicitly considered a student's race.[144] Transfer plans, for example, allowed students to shift from a school in which they were in the racial majority to a school in which they would be in a racial minority. Some districts, such as Richmond, California, and Buffalo, New York, permitted only "one-way" transfers, in which only black students attending predominantly black schools were permitted to transfer to designated receiver schools.[145] Fifty-three of the 125 studied districts used transfers as a component of their plans.[146]

At the state level, 46 States and Puerto Rico have adopted policies that encourage or require local school districts to enact interdistrict or intradistrict open choice plans. Eight of those States condition approval of transfers to another school or district on whether the transfer will produce increased racial integration. Eleven other States require local boards to deny transfers that are not in compliance with the local school board's desegregation plans.[147]

Arkansas, for example, provides by statute that "[n]o student may transfer to a nonresident district where the percentage of enrollment for the student's race exceeds that percentage in the student's resident district."[148] An Ohio statute provides, in respect to student choice, that each school district must establish "[p]rocedures to ensure that an appropriate racial balance is maintained in the district schools."[149] Ohio adds that a "district may object to the enrollment of a native student in an adjacent or other district in order to maintain an appropriate racial balance."[150]

A Connecticut statute states that its student choice program will seek to "preserve racial and ethnic balance."[151] Connecticut law requires each school district to submit racial group population figures to the State Board of Education.[152] Another Connecticut regulation provides that "[a]ny school in which the Proportion for the School falls outside of a range from 25 percentage points less to 25 percentage points more than the Comparable Proportion for the School District, shall be determined to be racially imbalanced."[153] A "racial imbalance" determination requires the district to submit a plan to correct the racial imbalance, which plan may include "mandatory pupil reassignment."[154]

Interpreting that State's Constitution, the Connecticut Supreme Court has held legally inadequate the reliance by a local school district solely upon some of the techniques Justice Kennedy today recommends (*e.g.*, reallocating resources, etc.).[155] The State Supreme Court wrote: "Despite the initiatives undertaken by the defendants to alleviate the severe racial and ethnic disparities among school districts, and despite the fact that the defendants did not intend to create or maintain these disparities, the disparities that continue to burden the education of the plaintiffs infringe upon their fundamental state constitutional right to a substantially equal educational opportunity."[156]

At a minimum, the plurality's views would threaten a surge of race-based litigation. Hundreds of state and federal statutes and regulations use racial classifications for educational or other purposes.[157] In many such instances, the contentious force of legal challenges to these classifications, meritorious or not, would displace earlier calm.

The wide variety of different integration plans that school districts use throughout the Nation suggests that the problem of racial segregation in schools, including *de facto* segregation, is difficult to solve. The fact that many such plans have used explicitly racial criteria suggests that such criteria have an important, sometimes necessary, role to play. The fact that the controlling opinion would make a school district's use of such criteria often unlawful (and the plurality's "colorblind" view would make such use always unlawful) suggests that today's opinion will require setting aside the laws of several States and many local communities.

As I have pointed out,[158] *de facto* resegregation is on the rise.[159] It is reasonable to conclude that such resegregation can create serious educational, social, and civic problems.[160] Given the conditions in which school boards work to set policy,[161] they may need all of the means presently at their disposal to combat those problems. Yet the plurality would deprive them of at least one tool that some districts now consider vital—the limited use of broad race-conscious student population ranges.

I use the words "may need" here deliberately. The plurality, or at least those who follow Justice Thomas' " 'color-blind' " approach,[162] may feel confident that, to end invidious discrimination, one must end *all* governmental use of race-conscious criteria including those with inclusive objectives.[163] By way of contrast, I do not claim to know how best to stop harmful discrimination; how best to create a society that includes all Americans; how best to overcome our serious problems of increasing *de facto* segregation, troubled inner city schooling, and poverty correlated with race. But, as a judge, I do know that the Constitution does not authorize judges to dictate solutions to these problems. Rather, the Constitution creates a democratic political system through which the people themselves must together find answers. And it is for them to debate how best to educate the Nation's children and how best to administer America's schools to achieve that aim. The Court should leave them to their work. And it is for them to decide, to quote the plurality's slogan, whether the best "way to stop discrimination on the basis of race is to stop discriminating on the basis of race."[164] That is why the Equal Protection Clause outlaws invidious discrimination, but does not similarly forbid all use of race-conscious criteria.

Until today, this Court understood the Constitution as affording the people, acting through their elected representatives, freedom to select the use of "race-conscious" criteria from among their available options.[165] Today, however, the Court restricts (and some Members would eliminate) that leeway. I fear the consequences of doing so for the law, for the schools, for the democratic process, and for America's efforts to create, out of its diversity, one Nation.

VI

Conclusions

To show that the school assignment plans here meet the requirements of the Constitution, I have written at exceptional length. But that length is necessary. I cannot refer to the history of the plans in these cases to justify the use of race-conscious criteria without describing that history in full. I cannot rely upon *Swann*'s statement that the use of race-conscious limits is permissible without showing, rather than simply asserting, that the statement represents a constitutional principle firmly rooted in federal and state law. Nor can I explain my disagreement with the Court's holding and the plurality's opinion, without offering a detailed account of the arguments they propound and the consequences they risk.

Thus, the opinion's reasoning is long. But its conclusion is short: The plans before us satisfy the requirements of the Equal Protection Clause. And it is the plurality's opinion, not this dissent that "fails to ground the result it would reach in law."[166]

Four basic considerations have led me to this view. *First*, the histories of Louisville and Seattle reveal complex circumstances and a long tradition of conscientious efforts by local school boards to resist racial segregation in public schools. Segregation at the time of *Brown* gave way to expansive remedies that included busing, which in turn gave rise to fears of white flight and resegregation. For decades now, these school boards have considered and adopted and revised assignment plans that sought to rely less upon race, to emphasize greater student choice, and to improve the conditions of all schools for all students, no matter the color of their skin, no matter where they happen to reside. The plans under review—which are less burdensome, more egalitarian, and more effective than prior plans—continue in that tradition. And their history reveals school district goals whose remedial, educational, and democratic elements are inextricably intertwined each with the others.[167]

Second, since this Court's decision in *Brown*, the law has consistently and unequivocally approved of both voluntary and compulsory race-conscious measures to combat segregated schools. The Equal Protection Clause, ratified following the Civil War, has always distinguished in practice between state action that excludes and thereby subordinates racial minorities and state action that seeks to bring together people of all races. From *Swann* to *Grutter*, this Court's decisions have emphasized this distinction, recognizing that the fate of race relations in this country depends upon unity among our children, "for unless our children begin to learn together, there is little hope that our people will ever learn to live together."[168]

Third, the plans before us, subjected to rigorous judicial review, are supported by compelling state interests and are narrowly tailored to accomplish those goals. Just as diversity in higher education was deemed compelling in *Grutter*, diversity in public primary and secondary schools—where there is even more to gain—must be, *a fortiori*, a compelling state interest. Even apart from *Grutter*, five Members of this Court agree that "avoiding racial isolation" and "achiev[ing] a diverse student population" remain today compelling interests.[169] These interests combine remedial, educational, and democratic objectives. For the reasons discussed above, however, I disagree with Justice Kennedy that Seattle and Louisville have not done enough to demonstrate that their present plans are necessary to continue upon the path set by *Brown*. These plans are *more* "narrowly tailored" than the race-conscious law school admissions criteria at issue in *Grutter*. Hence, their lawfulness follows *a fortiori* from this Court's prior decisions.[170]

Fourth, the plurality's approach risks serious harm to the law and for the Nation. Its view of the law rests either upon a denial of the distinction between exclusionary and inclusive use of race-conscious criteria in the context of the Equal Protection Clause, or upon such a rigid application of its "test" that the distinction loses practical significance. Consequently, the Court's decision today slows down and sets back the work of local school boards to bring about racially diverse schools.[171]

Indeed, the consequences of the approach the Court takes today are serious. Yesterday, the plans under review were lawful. Today, they are not. Yesterday, the citizens of this Nation could look for guidance to this Court's unanimous pronouncements concerning desegregation. Today, they cannot. Yesterday, school boards had available to them a full range of means to combat segregated schools. Today, they do not.

The Court's decision undermines other basic institutional principles as well. What has happened to *stare decisis*? The history of the plans before us, their educational importance, their highly limited use of race—all these and more—make clear that the compelling interest here is stronger than in *Grutter*. The plans here are more narrowly tailored than the law school admissions program there at issue. Hence, applying *Grutter*'s strict test, their lawfulness follows *a fortiori*. To hold to the contrary is to transform that test from "strict" to "fatal in fact"— the very opposite of what *Grutter* said. And what has happened to *Swann?* To *McDaniel?* To *Crawford?* To *Harris?* To *School Committee of Boston?* To *Seattle School Dist. No. 1?* After decades of vibrant life, they would all, under the plurality's logic, be written out of the law.

And what of respect for democratic local decisionmaking by States and school boards? For several decades this Court has rested its public school decisions upon *Swann*'s basic view that the Constitution grants local school districts a significant degree of leeway where the inclusive use of race-conscious criteria is at issue. Now localities will have to cope with the difficult problems they face (including resegregation) deprived of one means they may find necessary.

And what of law's concern to diminish and peacefully settle conflict among the Nation's people? Instead of accommodating different good-faith visions of our country and our Constitution, today's holding upsets settled expectations, creates legal uncertainty, and threatens to produce considerable further litigation, aggravating race-related conflict.

And what of the long history and moral vision that the Fourteenth Amendment itself embodies? The plurality cites in support those who argued in *Brown* against segregation, and Justice Thomas likens the approach that I have taken to that of segregation's defenders.[172] But segregation policies did not simply tell schoolchildren "where they could and could not go to school based on the color of their skin"[173]; they perpetuated a caste system rooted in the institutions of slavery and 80 years of legalized subordination. The lesson of history[174] is not that efforts to continue racial segregation are constitutionally indistinguishable from efforts to achieve racial integration. Indeed, it is a cruel distortion of history to compare Topeka, Kansas, in the

1950s to Louisville and Seattle in the modern day—to equate the plight of Linda Brown (who was ordered to attend a Jim Crow school) to the circumstances of Joshua McDonald (whose request to transfer to a school closer to home was initially declined). This is not to deny that there is a cost in applying "a state-mandated racial label."[175] But that cost does not approach, in degree or in kind, the terrible harms of slavery, the resulting caste system, and 80 years of legal racial segregation.

*   *   *

Finally, what of the hope and promise of *Brown?* For much of this Nation's history, the races remained divided. It was not long ago that people of different races drank from separate fountains, rode on separate buses, and studied in separate schools. In this Court's finest hour, *Brown* v. *Board of Education* challenged this history and helped to change it. For *Brown* held out a promise. It was a promise embodied in three Amendments designed to make citizens of slaves. It was the promise of true racial equality—not as a matter of fine words on paper, but as a matter of everyday life in the Nation's cities and schools. It was about the nature of a democracy that must work for all Americans. It sought one law, one Nation, one people, not simply as a matter of legal principle but in terms of how we actually live.

Not everyone welcomed this Court's decision in *Brown*. Three years after that decision was handed down, the Governor of Arkansas ordered state militia to block the doors of a white schoolhouse so that black children could not enter. The President of the United States dispatched the 101st Airborne Division to Little Rock, Arkansas, and federal troops were needed to enforce a desegregation decree.[176] Today, almost 50 years later, attitudes toward race in this Nation have changed dramatically. Many parents, white and black alike, want their children to attend schools with children of different races. Indeed, the very school districts that once spurned integration now strive for it. The long history of their efforts reveals the complexities and difficulties they have faced. And in light of those challenges, they have asked us not to take from their hands the instruments they have used to rid their schools of racial segregation, instruments that they believe are needed to overcome the problems of cities divided by race and poverty. The plurality would decline their modest request.

The plurality is wrong to do so. The last half-century has witnessed great strides toward racial equality, but we have not yet realized the promise of *Brown*. To invalidate the plans under review is to threaten the promise of *Brown*. The plurality's position, I fear, would break that promise. This is a decision that the Court and the Nation will come to regret.

I must dissent.

APPENDIX A

Resegregation Trends

Percentage of Black Students in 90–100 Percent Nonwhite and Majority Nonwhite Public Schools by Region, 1950–1954 to 2000, Fall Enrollment

Region	1950–1954	1960–1961	1968	1972	1976	1980	1989	1999	2000
Percentage in 90–100% Nonwhite Schools									
Northeast	—	40	42.7	46.9	51.4	48.7	49.8	50.2	51.2
Border	100	59	60.2	54.7	42.5	37.0	33.7	39.7	39.6
South	100	100	77.8	24.7	22.4	23.0	26.0	31.1	30.9
Midwest	53	56	58.0	57.4	51.1	43.6	40.1	45.0	46.3
West	—	27	50.8	42.7	36.3	33.7	26.7	29.9	29.5
U. S.			64.3	38.7	35.9	33.2	33.8	37.4	37.4
Percentage in 50–100% Nonwhite Schools									
Northeast	—	62	66.8	69.9	72.5	79.9	75.4	77.5	78.3
Border	100	69	71.6	67.2	60.1	59.2	58.0	64.8	67.0
South	100	100	80.9	55.3	54.9	57.1	59.3	67.3	69.0
Midwest	78	80	77.3	75.3	70.3	69.5	69.4	67.9	73.3
West	—	69	72.2	68.1	67.4	66.8	67.4	76.7	75.3
U. S.			76.6	63.6	62.4	62.9	64.9	70.1	71.6

Source: C. Clotfelter, *After Brown: The Rise and Retreat of School Desegregation* 56 (2004) (Table 2.1).

Changes in the Percentage of White Students in Schools Attended by the Average Black Student by State, 1970–2003 (includes States with 5% or greater enrollment of black students in 1970 and 1980)

	% White	% White Students in School of Average Black Student				Change		
	2003	1970	1980	1991	2003	1970–1980	1980–1991	1991–2003
Alabama	60	33	38	35	30	5	-3	-5
Arkansas	70	43	47	44	36	4	-3	-8
California	33	26	28	27	22	2	-1	-5
Connecticut	68	44	40	35	32	-4	-5	-3
Delaware	57	47	69	65	49	22	-4	-16
Florida	51	43	51	43	34	8	-8	-9
Georgia	52	35	38	35	30	3	-3	-5
Illinois	57	15	19	20	19	4	1	-1
Indiana	82	32	39	47	41	7	8	-6
Kansas	76	52	59	58	51	7	-1	-7
Kentucky	87	49	74	42	65	25	-2	-7
Louisiana	48	31	33	32	27	2	-1	-5
Maryland	50	30	35	29	23	5	-6	-6
Massachusetts	75	48	50	45	38	2	-5	-7
Michigan	73	22	23	22	22	1	-1	0
Mississippi	47	30	29	30	26	-1	1	-4
Missouri	78	21	34	40	33	13	6	-7
Nebraska	80	33	66	62	49	33	-4	-13
New Jersey	58	32	26	26	25	-6	0	-1
New York	54	29	23	20	18	-6	-3	-2
Nevada	51	56	68	62	38	12	-6	-24
N. Carolina	58	49	54	51	40	5	-3	-11
Ohio	79	28	43	41	32	15	-2	-9
Oklahoma	61	42	58	51	42	16	-7	-9
Pennsylvania	76	28	29	31	30	1	2	-1
S. Carolina	54	41	43	42	39	2	-1	-3
Tennessee	73	29	38	36	32	9	-2	-4
Texas	39	31	35	35	27	4	0	-8
Virginia	61	42	47	46	41	5	-1	-5
Wisconsin	79	26	45	39	29	19	-6	-10

Source: G. Orfield & C. Lee, Racial Transformation and the Changing Nature of Segregation 18 (Table 8) (Jan. 2006),(Civil Rights Project), online at http://www.civilrightspro ject.harvard .edu/research/deseg/Racial_Transformation.pdf.

Percentage of White Students in Schools Attended
by the Average Black Student, 1968–2000

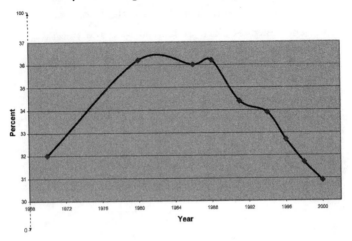

Source: Modified from E. Frankenberg, C. Lee, & G. Orfield, *A Multiracial Society with Segregated Schools: Are We Losing the Dream?*, p. 30, fig. 5 (Jan. 2003), online at http://www.civilrights project.harvard.edu/research/reseg03/AreWeLosingtheDream.pdf (Frankenberg, Lee, & Orfield) (using U.S. Dept. of Education and National Center for Education Statistics Common Core data).

Breaking the Promise of Brown

Percentage of Students in Minority Schools by Race, 2000–2001

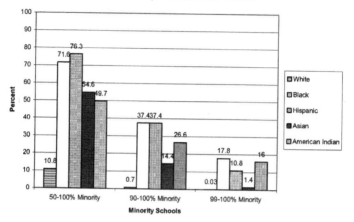

Source: Id., at 28, fig. 4.

APPENDIX B

Sources for Parts I–A and I–B

Part I–A: Seattle
Section 1. Segregation
¶1 C. Schmid & W. McVey, Growth and Distribution of Minority Races in Seattle, Washington, 3, 7–9 (1964); F. Hanawalt & R. Williams, The History of Desegregation in Seattle Public Schools, 1954–1981, pp. 1–7 (1981) (hereinafter Hanawalt); Taylor, The Civil Rights Movement in the American West: Black Protest in Seattle, 1960–1970, 80 J. Negro Hist. 1, 2–3 (1995); A. Siqueland, Without A Court Order: The Desegregation of Seattle's Schools 10 (1981) (hereinafter Siqueland); D. Pieroth, Desegregating the Public Schools, Seattle, Washington, 1954–1968, p. 6 (Dissertation Draft 1979) (hereinafter Pieroth).

Section 2. Preliminary Challenges, 1956 to 1969
¶1 Pieroth 32, 41; Hanawalt 4.
¶2 Hanawalt 11–13.
¶3 *Id.*, at 5, 13, 27.

Section 3. The NAACP's First Legal Challenge
and Seattle's Response, 1969 to 1977
¶1 Complaint in Adams v. *Forbes Bottomly*, Civ. No. 6704 (WD Wash., 1969), pp. 10–11.

¶2 *Id.,* at 10, 14–15.

¶3 Planning and Evaluation Dept., Seattle Public Schools, The Plan Adopted by the Seattle School Board to Desegregate Fifth, Sixth, Seventh, and Eighth Grade Pupils in the Garfield, Lincoln, and Roosevelt High School Districts by September, 1971, pp. 6, 11 (on file with the University of Washington Library); *see generally* Siqueland 12–15; Hanawalt 18–20.

¶4 Siqueland 5, 7, 21.

Section 4. The NAACP's Second Legal Challenge, 1977

¶1 Administrative Complaint in Seattle Branch, *NAACP v. Seattle School Dist. No. 1*, pp. 2–3 (OCR, Apr. 22, 1977) (OCR Complaint) (filed with Court as Exhibit in *Seattle School Dist. No. 1*, 458 U. S. 457); see generally Siqueland 23–24.

¶2 Memorandum of Agreement between Seattle School District No. 1 of King Cty., Washington, and the OCR (June 9, 1978) (filed with the Court as Exh. A to Kiner Affidavit in Seattle School Dist. No. 1, *supra.*

Section 5. The Seattle Plan: Mandatory Busing, 1978 to 1988

¶1 See generally *Seattle School Dist. No. 1, supra,* at 461; Seattle Public Schools Desegregation Planning Office, Proposed Alternative Desegregation Plans: Options for Eliminating Racial Imbalance by the 1979-80 School Year (Sept. 1977) (filed with the Court as Exh. B to Roe Affidavit in *Seattle School Dist. No. 1, supra*); Hanawalt 36–38, 40; Siqueland 3, 184, Table 4.

¶2 *Id.,* at 151–152; Hanawalt 37–38; *Seattle School Dist. No. 1, supra,* at 461; Complaint and Motion to Dismiss or Affirm in *Seattle School Dist. No. 1, supra.*

¶3 *Seattle School Dist. No. 1, supra,* at 461; Hanawalt 40.

¶4 See generally *Seattle School Dist. No. 1, supra.*

Section 6. Student Choice, 1988 to 1998

¶1 L. Kohn, *Priority Shift: The Fate of Mandatory Busing for School Desegregation in Seattle and the Nation* 27–30, 32 (Mar. 1996).

¶2 *Id.,* at 32–34.

Section 7. The Current Plan, 1999 to the Present

¶1 App. in No. 05–908, p. 84a; Brief for Respondents in No. 05–908, pp. 5–7; 426 F. 3d 1162, 1169–1170 (CA9 2005) (en banc) (*Parents Involved VII*).

¶2 App. in No. 05–908, at 39–42; Research, Evaluation and Assessment, Student Information Services Office, Seattle Public Schools Data Profile: District Summary December 2005, online at http://www.seattleschools.org/area/siso/disprof/2005/DP05all.pdf; Brief for Respond-ents in No. 05–908, at 9–10, 47; App. in No. 05–908,at 309a; School Board Report, School Choices and Assignments 2005–2006 School Year (Apr. 2005), online at http://www.seattleschools.org/area/facilties-plan/ Choice/05-06AppsChoicesBoardApril2005final.pdf.

¶3 *Parents Involved in Community Schools* v. *Seattle School Dist., No. 1*, 149 Wash. 2d 660, 72 P. 3d 151 (2003); 137 F. Supp. 2d 1224 (2001); 426 F. 3d 1162 (CA9 2005) (en banc) (*Parents Involved VII*).

Part I–B: Louisville
Section 1. Before the Lawsuit, 1954 to 1972
¶1 Hampton v. *Jefferson Cty., Bd. of Ed.*, 72 F. Supp. 2d 753, 756, and nn. 2, 4, 5 (WD Ky. 1999) (*Hampton I*).

Section 2. Court-Imposed Guidelines and Busing, 1972 to 1991
¶1 Hampton I, *supra*, at 757–758, 762; *Newburg Area Council, Inc.* v. *Board of Ed. of Jefferson Cty.*, 489 F. 2d 925 (CA6 1973), vacated and remanded, 418 U. S. 918 (1974), reinstated with modifications, 510 F. 2d 1358 (CA6 1974) (*per curiam*); Judgment and Findings of Fact and Conclusions of Law in *Newburg Area Council, Inc.*v. *Board of Ed., of Jefferson Cty.*, Nos. 7045 and 7291 (WD Ky., July 30, 1975) (1975 Judgment and Findings).

¶2 *Id.*, at 2, 3, and Attachment 1.

¶3 *Id.*, at 4–16.

¶4 Memorandum Opinion and Order in *Haycraft* v. *Board of Ed. of Jefferson Cty.*, Nos. 7045 and 7291, (WD Ky., June 16, 1978), pp. 1, 2, 4, 18 (1978 Memo & Order).

¶5 Memorandum Opinion and Order, *Haycraft* v. *Board of Ed. of Jefferson Cty.*, Nos. 7045 and 7291 (WD Ky., Sept. 24, 1985), p. 3; Memorandum from Donald W. Ingwerson, Superintendent, to the Board of Education, Jefferson Cty. Public School Dist., pp. 1, 3, 5 (Apr. 4, 1984) (1984 Memorandum); Memorandum from Donald W. Ingwerson, Superintendent, to the Board of Education, Jefferson County Public School District, pp. 4–5 (Dec. 19, 1991) (1991 Memorandum).

Section 3. Student Choice and Project Renaissance, 1991 to 1996
¶1 1991 Memorandum 1–4, 7–11 (Stipulated Exh. 72); Brief for Respondents in No. 05–915, P. 12, n. 13.
¶2 1991 Memorandum 14–16.
¶3 *Id.,* at 11, 14–15.
¶4 *Id.,* at 15–16; Memorandum from Stephen W. Daeschner, Superintendent, to the Board of Education, Jefferson Cty. Public School Dist., p. 2 (Aug. 6, 1996) (1996 Memorandum).

Section 4. The Current Plan: Project
Renaissance Modified, 1996 to 2003
¶1 1996 Memorandum 1–4; Brief for Respondents in No. 05–915, at 12, and n. 13.
¶2 1996 Memorandum 4–7, and Attachment 2; *Hampton I, supra,* at 768.
¶3 1996 Memorandum 5–8; *Hampton I, supra,* at 768, n. 30.
¶4 *Hampton v. Jefferson Cty. Bd. of Ed.,* 102 F. Supp. 2d 358, 359, 363, 370, 377 (WD Ky. 2000) (*Hampton II*).
¶5 *Id.,* at 380–381.

Section 5. The Current Lawsuit, 2003 to the Present
¶1 *McFarland v. Jefferson Cty. Public Schools,* 330 F. Supp. 2d 834 (WD Ky. 2004); *McFarland v. Jefferson Cty. Public Schools,* 416 F. 3d 513 (2005); Memorandum from Stephen W. Daeschner, Superintendent, to the Board of Education, Jefferson Cty. Public School Dist., 3–4 (Apr. 2, 2001).

NOTES TO JUSTICE BREYER'S DISSENT IN
THE RESEGREGATION CASES

1. 347 U.S. 483 (1954).

2. 347 U.S., at 493.

3. *See, e.g., Columbus Bd. of Ed.* v. *Penick*, 443 U.S. 449, 455, n. 3 (1979); *Davis* v. *Board of School Comm'rs of Mobile Cty.*, 402 U.S. 33, 37–38 (1971); *Green* v. *School Bd. of New Kent Cty.*, 391 U.S. 430, 441–442 (1968).

4. *Swann* v. *Charlotte-Mecklenburg Bd. of Ed.*, 402 U.S. 1, 16 (1971) (emphasis added).

5. *See* F. Welch & A. Light, *New Evidence on School Desegregation* V (1987) (hereinafter Welch) (prepared for the Commission on Civil Rights) (reviewing a sample of 125 school districts, constituting 20% of national public school enrollment, that had experimented with nearly 300 different plans over 18 years).

6. *Id.*, at 21.

7. *Ibid.*

8. *See* Appendix A, *infra.*

9. *See generally Washington* v. *Seattle School Dist. No. 1*, 458 U.S. 457, 461–466 (1982).

10. *Id.*, at 462.

11. *Id.*, at 464.

12. *Id.*, at 470.

13. *Ante*, at 6, n. 4 (concurring opinion).

14. *See Yick Wo* v. *Hopkins*, 118 U.S. 356, 373–374 (1886).

15. *Compare ante*, at 12 (opinion of the Court) ("[T]he Seattle public schools *have never shown* that they were ever segregated by law" (emphasis added)), *with ante* at 29–30 (plurality opinion) (assuming "the Seattle school district was never segregated by law," but seeming to concede that a school district with *de jure* segregation need not be subject to a court order to be allowed to engage in race-based remedial measures).

16. *See, e.g.*, Coleman, *Desegregation of the Public Schools in Kentucky—The Second Year After the Supreme Court's Decision*, 25 J. Negro Educ. 254, 256, 261 (1956) (40 of Kentucky's 180 school districts began desegregation without court orders); Branton, *Little Rock Revisited: Desegregation to Resegregation*, 52 J. Negro Educ. 250, 251 (1983) (similar in Arkansas); Bullock & Rodgers, *Coercion to Compliance: Southern School Districts and School Desegregation Guidelines*, 38 J. Politics 987, 991 (1976) (similar in Georgia); *McDaniel* v. *Barresi*, 402 U.S. 39, 40, n. 1 (1971) (Clarke County, Georgia). *See also* Letter from Robert F. Kennedy, Attorney General, to John F. Kennedy, President (Jan. 24, 1963) (hereinafter Kennedy Report), available at http://www.gilderlehrman.org/search/collection_pdfs/05/63/0/05630.pdf (all Internet materials as visited June 26, 2007, and available in Clerk of Court's case file) (reporting successful efforts by the Government to induce voluntary desegregation).

17. *But see ante*, at 12–13, 17, n. 12.

18. *See id.*, at 12, 29–30.

19. *See McDaniel, supra*, at 41.

20. *But see ante*, at 29.

21. *Comfort* v. *Lynn School Comm.*, 418 F. 3d 1, 28 (CA1 2005) (Boudin, C. J., concurring) (citing *United States* v. *Lopez*, 514 U.S. 549, 581 (1995) (Kennedy, J., concurring)), cert. denied, 546 U.S. 1061 (2005).

22. *Swann* v. *Charlotte-Mecklenburg Bd. of Ed.*, 402 U.S. 1, 16 (1971).

23. *Dickerson* v. *United States*, 530 U.S. 428, 443 (2000) (internal quotation marks omitted); *Mitchell* v. *United States*, 526 U.S. 314, 330 (1999); *id.*, at 331, 332 (Scalia, J., dissenting) (citing " 'wide acceptance

in the legal culture'" as "adequate reason not to overrule" prior cases).

24. 402 U.S. 43, 45 (1971).

25. 439 U.S. 1380, 1383 (1978) (opinion in chambers) (emphasis in original).

26. See Barresi v. Browne, 226 Ga. 456, 456–459, 175 S. E. 2d 649, 650–651 (1970).

27. See McDaniel, 402 U.S., at 41.

28. Brief for Respondents in McDaniel, O.T. 1970, No. 420, p. 25.

29. Compare ante, at 29, with supra, at 6–9.

30. See McDaniel, 402 U.S., at 41 ("[S]teps will almost invariably require that students be assigned 'differently because of their race.' . . . Any other approach would freeze the status quo that is the very target of all desegregation processes.").

31. 444 U.S. 130, 148–149 (1979).

32. See id., at 152 (opinion of Stewart, J.). See also, e.g., Crawford v. Board of Ed. of Los Angeles, 458 U.S. 527, 535–536 (1982) ("[S]tate courts of California continue to have an obligation under state law to order segregated school districts to use voluntary desegregation techniques, whether or not there has been a finding of intentional segregation. . . . [S]chool districts themselves retain a state-law obligation to take reasonably feasible steps to desegregate, and they remain free to adopt reassignment and busing plans to effectuate desegregation" (emphasis added)); School Comm. of Boston v. Board of Education, 389 U.S. 572 (1968) (per curiam) (dismissing for want of a federal question a challenge to a voluntary statewide integration plan using express racial criteria).

33. 39 Ill. 2d 593, 597–598, 237 N. E. 2d 498, 501 (1968) (citations omitted) (citing decisions from the high courts of Pennsylvania, Massachusetts, New Jersey, California, New York, and Connecticut, and from the Courts of Appeals for the First, Second, Fourth, and Sixth Circuits). See also, e.g., Offerman v. Nitkowski, 378 F. 2d 22, 24 (CA2 1967); Deal v. Cincinnati Bd. of Ed., 369 F. 2d 55, 61 (CA6 1966), cert. denied, 389 U.S. 847 (1967); Springfield School Comm. v. Barksdale, 348 F. 2d 261, 266 (CA1 1965); Pennsylvania Human Relations Comm'n v. Chester School Dist., 427 Pa. 157, 164, 233 A. 2d 290, 294 (1967); Booker v.

Board of Ed. of Plainfield, Union Cty., 45 N. J. 161, 170, 212 A. 2d 1, 5 (1965); *Jackson v. Pasadena City School Dist.*, 59 Cal. 2d 876, 881–882, 382 P. 2d 878, 881–882 (1963) (in bank).

34. *Citizens for Better Ed. v. Goose Creek Consol. Independent School Dist.*, 719 S. W. 2d 350, 352–353 (Ct. App. Tex. 1986) (citing *Swann* and *North Carolina Bd. of Ed.*), appeal dism'd for want of a substantial federal question, 484 U.S. 804 (1987).

35. 610 F. 2d 661, 662–664 (1979).

36. 610 F. 2d, at 663–664. See also, *e.g., Darville v. Dade County School Bd.*, 497 F. 2d 1002, 1004–1006 (CA5 1974); *State ex rel. Citizens Against Mandatory Bussing v. Brooks*, 80 Wash. 2d 121, 128–129, 492 P. 2d 536, 541–542 (1972) (en banc), overruled on other grounds, *Cole v. Webster*, 103 Wash. 2d 280, 692 P. 2d 799 (1984) (en banc); *School Comm. of Springfield v. Board of Ed.*, 362 Mass. 417, 428–429 287 N. E. 2d 438, 447–448 (1972).

37. *See, e.g.*, 20 U.S. C. §6311(b)(2)(C)(v) (No Child Left Behind Act); §1067 *et seq.* (authorizing aid to minority institutions).

38. *See, e.g.*, Exec. Order No. 10925, 26 Fed. Reg. 1977 (1961) (President Kennedy); Exec. Order No. 11246, 30 Fed. Reg. 12319 (1965) (President Johnson); Sugrue, *Breaking Through: The Troubled Origins of Affirmative Action in the Workplace*, in *Colorlines: Affirmative Action, Immigration, and Civil Rights Options for America* 31 (Skretny ed. 2001) (describing President Nixon's lobbying for affirmative action plans, *e.g.*, the Philadelphia Plan); White, *Affirmative Action's Alamo: Gerald Ford Returns to Fight Once More for Michigan, Time*, Aug. 23, 1999, p. 48 (reporting on President Ford's support for affirmative action); Schuck, *Affirmative Action: Past, Present, and Future*, 20 *Yale L. & Pol'y Rev.* 1, 50 (2002) (describing President Carter's support for affirmation action).

39. *See* Welch 83–91.

40. *See Slaughter-House Cases*, 16 Wall. 36, 71 (1872) ("[N]o one can fail to be impressed with the one pervading purpose found in [all the Reconstruction amendments] . . . we mean the freedom of the slave race"); *Strauder v. West Virginia*, 100 U.S. 303, 306 (1879) ("[The Fourteenth Amendment] is one of a series of constitutional provisions

having a common purpose; namely, securing to a race recently emancipated . . . all the civil rights that the superior race enjoy").

41. *See generally* R. Sears, *A Utopian Experiment in Kentucky: Integration and Social Equality at Berea, 1866–1904* (1996) (describing federal funding, through the Freedman's Bureau, of race-conscious school integration programs). *See also* R. Fischer, *The Segregation Struggle in Louisiana 1862–77*, p. 51 (1974) (describing the use of race-conscious remedies); Harlan, *Desegregation in New Orleans Public Schools During Reconstruction*, 67 *Am. Hist. Rev.* 663, 664 (1962) (same); W. Vaughn, *Schools for All: The Blacks and Public Education in the South*, 1865–1877, pp. 111–116 (1974) (same).

42. See *Gratz* v. *Bollinger*, 539 U.S. 244, 301 (2003) (Ginsburg, J., dissenting); *Adarand Constructors, Inc.* v. *Peña*, 515 U.S. 200, 243 (1995) (Stevens, J., dissenting).

43. *See Wygant* v. *Jackson Board of Education*, 476 U.S. 267, 274 (1986); *Fullilove* v. *Klutznick*, 448 U.S. 448, 507 (1980).

44. *See supra*, at 22–24.

45. *See supra*, at 19–20. *See also* Kennedy Report.

46. 438 U.S. 265 (1978).

47. *See ante*, at 11–12, 31–32, n. 16, 34–35 (citing *Adarand, supra,* at 227; *Johnson* v. *California*, 543 U.S. 499, 505 (2005); *Grutter* v. *Bollinger*, 539 U.S. 306, 326 (2003)).

48. *Ante*, at 31, n. 16 (quoting *Adarand*, 515 U.S., at 227).

49. *Ibid.*

50. *See* 539 U.S., at 326.

51. *See, e.g., Adarand, supra; Gratz, supra; Grutter, supra.*

52. *Adarand, supra*, at 228 (internal quotation marks omitted).

53. *Id.*, at 229–230 (internal quotation marks omitted).

54. *Id.*, at 237 (quoting *Fullilove* v. *Klutznick*, 448 U.S., at 519 (Marshall, J., concurring in judgment)).

55. See *Gomillion* v. *Lightfoot*, 364 U.S. 339, 343–344 (1960) (admonishing that, 'in dealing with claims under broad provisions of the Constitution, which derive content by an interpretive process of inclusion and exclusion, it is imperative that generalizations, based on and qualified by the concrete situations that gave rise to them, must not be applied out of context in disregard of variant controlling facts').

56. 539 U.S., at 326–327.

57. *See ante*, at 34–36.

58. 539 U.S., at 327 (citing *Gomillion* v. *Lightfoot,* 364 U.S. 339, 343–344 (1960)).

59. *See, e.g., Strauder* v. *West Virginia,* 100 U.S. 303 (1880); *Yick Wo* v. *Hopkins,* 118 U.S. 356 (1886); *Brown,* 347 U.S. 483; *Loving* v. *Virginia,* 388 U.S. 1 (1967); *Regents of Univ. of Cal.* v. *Bakke,* 438 U.S. 265 (1978); *Batson* v. *Kentucky,* 476 U.S. 79 (1986); *Richmond* v. *J. A. Croson Co.,* 488 U.S. 469 (1989); *Shaw* v. *Reno,* 509 U.S. 630 (1993); *Adarand Constructors, Inc.* v. *Peña,* 515 U.S. 200 (1995); *Grutter, supra; Gratz* v. *Bollinger,* 539 U.S. 244 (2003); *Johnson* v. *California,* 543 U.S. 499 (2005).

60. *Compare Wessmann* v. *Gittens,* 160 F. 3d 790, 809–810 (CA1 1998) (Boudin, J., concurring), *with Comfort,* 418 F. 3d, at 28–29 (Boudin, C. J., concurring).

61. *See* Research, Evaluation and Assessment, Student Information Services Office, District Summaries 1999–2005, available at http://www.seattleschools.org/area/siso/disprof/2005/DP05 all.pdf.

62. *See* 426 F. 3d 1162, 1193–1194 (2005) (Kozinski, J., concurring) ("That a student is denied the school of his choice may be disappointing, but it carries no racial stigma and says nothing at all about that individual's aptitude or ability"). That judge is not alone. Cf. *Gratz, supra,* at 301 (Ginsburg, J., dissenting); *Adarand, supra,* at 243 (Stevens, J., dissenting); Carter, *When Victims Happen To Be Black,* 97 *Yale L. J.* 420, 433–434 (1988).

63. *See ante,* at 11–12 (Thomas, J., concurring); *ante,* at 3, 17 (opinion of Kennedy, J.).

64. *Cf. ante,* at 17–18 (opinion of Kennedy, J.).

65. *See Gratz, supra,* at 301 (Ginsburg, J., joined by Souter, J., dissenting); *Adarand, supra,* at 242–249 (Stevens, J., joined by Ginsburg, J., dissenting); 426 F. 3d, at 1193–1194 (Kozinski, J., concurring).

66. *See, e.g., Bakke,* 438 U.S., at 290 (opinion of Powell, J.).

67. *See* Part I, *supra,* at 4; Appendix A, *infra. See also ante,* at 17 (opinion of Kennedy, J.) ("This Nation has a moral and ethical obligation to fulfill its historic commitment to creating an integrated society that ensures equal opportunity for all of its children").

68. *Cf. Grutter*, 539 U.S., at 345 (Ginsburg, J., concurring).

69. *See, e.g.*, Powell, *Living and Learning: Linking Housing and Education, in Pursuit of a Dream Deferred: Linking Housing and Education Policy* 15, 35 (J. Powell, G. Kearney, & V. Kay eds. 2001) (hereinafter Powell); Hallinan, *Diversity Effects on Student Outcomes: Social Science Evidence*, 59 *Ohio St. L. J.* 733, 741–742 (1998) (hereinafter Hallinan).

70. *See, e.g.*, D. Armor, Forced Justice (1995). *See also ante*, at 15–17 (Thomas, J., concurring).

71. *See* Powell 35.

72. *Ibid.*

73. *See* Hallinan 741–742.

74. *See, e.g.*, Schofield, *Review of Research on School Desegregation's Impact on Elementary and Secondary School Students*, in *Handbook of Research on Multicultural Education* 597, 606–607 (J. Banks & C. Banks eds. 1995). *Cf.* W. Bowen & D. Bok, *The Shape of the River* 118 (1998) (hereinafter Bowen & Bok).

75. *Swann*, 402 U.S., at 16.

76. *See, e.g.*, Hallinan 745; Quillian & Campbell, *Beyond Black and White: The Present and Future of Multiracial Friendship Segregation*, 68 *Am. Sociological Rev.* 540, 541 (2003) (hereinafter Quillian & Campbell); Dawkins & Braddock, *The Continuing Significance of Desegregation: School Racial Composition and African American Inclusion in American Society*, 63 *J. Negro Ed.* 394, 401–403 (1994) (hereinafter Dawkins & Braddock); Wells & Crain, *Perpetuation Theory and the Long-Term Effects of School Desegregation*, 64 *Rev. Educational Research* 531, 550 (1994) (hereinafter Wells & Crain).

77. *See, e.g.*, Schofield, *School Desegregation and Intergroup Relations*, in 17 *Review of Research in Education* 356 (G. Grant ed. 1991). *See also ante*, at 22–23 (Thomas, J., concurring).

78. Hallinan 745. *See also* Quillian & Campbell 541. *Cf.* Bowen & Bok 155.

79. Dawkins & Braddock 401–403; Wells & Crain 550.

80. Dawkins & Braddock 403.

81. *See, e.g., Swann, supra*, at 16; *Seattle School Dist. No. 1*, 458 U.S., at 472–473.

82. See 539 U.S., at 330 (recognizing that Michigan Law School's race-conscious admissions policy "promotes cross-racial understanding, helps to break down racial stereotypes, and enables [students] to better understand persons of different races," and pointing out that "the skills needed in today's increasingly global marketplace can only be developed through exposure to widely diverse people, cultures, ideas, and viewpoints" (internal quotation marks omitted; alteration in original).

83. *Milliken* v. *Bradley,* 418 U.S. 717, 783 (1974) (dissenting opinion).

84. 339 U.S. 629 (1950).

85. 339 U.S. 637(1950).

86. R. Kluger, *Simple Justice: The History of Brown v. Board of Education and Black America's Struggle for Equality,* p. x (1975) (arguing that perhaps no other Supreme Court case has "affected more directly the minds, hearts, and daily lives of so many Americans"); Patterson, *Brown v. Board of Education* xxvii (2001) (identifying *Brown* as "the most eagerly awaited and dramatic judicial decision of modern times"). *See also Parents Involved VII,*426 F. 3d, at 1194 (Kozinski, J., concurring); Strauss, *Discriminatory Intent and the Taming of* Brown, 56 *U. Chi. L. Rev.* 935, 937 (1989) (calling *Brown* "the Supreme Court's greatest anti-discrimination decision"); Brief for United States as *Amicus Curiae* in *Brown,* 347 U.S. 483; Dudziak, *Brown* as a Cold War Case, 91 *J. Am. Hist.* 32 (2004); *A Great Decision, Hindustan Times* (New Dehli, May 20, 1954), p. 5; *USA Takes Positive Step, West African Pilot* (Lagos, May 22, 1954), p. 2 (stating that *Brown* is an acknowledgment that the "United States should set an example for all other nations by taking the lead in removing from its national life all signs and traces of racial intolerance, arrogance or discrimination").

87. *Ante,* at 17–18.

88. *Ante,* at 23 (plurality opinion).

89. *See supra,* at 7, 14.

90. *Ante,* at 12, 13.

91. *Supra,* at 19–20.

92. *Ante,* at 28.

93. Compare, *e.g., Green,* 391 U.S., at 437–438 ("School boards . . .

operating state-compelled dual systems" have an "affirmative duty to take whatever steps might be necessary to convert to a unitary system in which racial discrimination would be eliminated root and branch"), with, *e.g.*, *Milliken*, 418 U.S., at 745 (the Constitution does not impose a duty to desegregate upon districts that have not been "shown to have committed any constitutional violation").

94. *See, e.g., Freeman* v. *Pitts*, 503 U.S. 467, 495 (1992).

95. *Ante*, at 29.

96. 503 U.S., at 495. See also *ante*, at 15 (opinion of Kennedy, J.).

97. *See ante*, at 15–17, 23 (concurring opinion).

98. *Cf. ante*, at 15–17 (opinion of Thomas, J.) (citing Armor & Rossell, Desegregation and Resegregation in the Public Schools, in Beyond the Color Line 239 (A. Thernstrom & S. Thernstrom eds. 2002); Brief for Armor *et al.* as *Amici Curiae*, with Rosen, Perhaps Not All Affirmative Action is Created Equal, *N.Y. Times*, June 11, 2006 (quoting David Armor as commenting " '[w]e did find the [racial] achievement gap changing *significantly*' " and acknowledging that he " 'did find a modest association for math but not reading in terms of racial composition and achievement, but there's a big state variation' " (emphasis added)).

99. *Cf. Miller* v. *Johnson*, 515 U.S. 900, 920 (1995).

100. *Grutter*, 539 U.S., at 388 (Kennedy, J., dissenting).

101. *Cf. id.,* at 390 (Kennedy, J., dissenting) (expressing concern about "narrow fluctuation band[s]").

102. *See id.,* at 335 ("Properly understood, a 'quota' is a program in which a certain fixed number or proportion of opportunities are 'reserved exclusively for certain minority groups'" (quoting *Croson*, 488 U.S., at 496)).

103. *See Grutter, supra*, at 393 (Kennedy, J., dissenting) (allowing consideration of race only if it does "not become a predominant factor").

104. *See, e.g., North Carolina Bd. of Ed.* v. *Swann*, 402 U.S. 43, 46 (1971) (no "absolute prohibition against [the] use" of mathematical ratios as a "starting point"); *Swann*, 402 U.S., at 24–25 (approving the use of a ratio reflecting "the racial composition of the whole school system" as a "useful starting point," but not as an "inflexible

requirement"). *Cf. United States* v. *Montgomery County Bd. of Ed.*, 395 U.S. 225, 232 (1969) (approving a lower court desegregation order that "provided that the [school] board must move toward a goal under which 'in each school the ratio of white to Negro faculty members is substantially the same as it is throughout the system,'" and "immediately" requiring "[t]he ratio of Negro to white teachers" in each school to be equal to "the ratio of Negro to white teachers in . . . the system as a whole").

105. *See Grutter, supra*, at 341.

106. *See, e.g., Swann, supra*, at 26–27; *Montgomery Co. Bd. of Ed., supra*, at 232.

107. *Cf. Wygant*, 476 U.S., at 283.

108. *See* Parts I–A and I–B, *supra*, at 6–18.

109. *See Milliken*, 418 U.S., at 741–42 ("No single tradition in public education is more deeply rooted than local control over the operation of schools; local autonomy has long been thought essential both to the maintenance of community concern and support for public schools and to quality of the educational process"). *See also San Antonio Independent School Dist.* v. *Rodriguez*, 411 U.S. 1, 49–50 (1973) (extolling local control for "the opportunity it offers for participation in the decisionmaking process that determines how . . . local tax dollars will be spent. Each locality is free to tailor local programs to local needs. Pluralism also affords some opportunity for experimentation, innovation, and a healthy competition for educational excellence"); *Epperson* v. *Arkansas*, 393 U.S. 97, 104 (1968) ("Judicial interposition in the operation of the public school system of the Nation raises problems requiring care and restraint. . . . By and large, public education in our Nation is committed to the control of state and local authorities"); *Brown* v. *Board of Education*, 349 U.S. 294, 299 (1955) (*Brown II*) ("Full implementation of these constitutional principles may require solution of varied local school problems. School authorities have the primary responsibility for elucidating, assessing, and solving these problems; courts will have to consider whether the action of school authorities constitutes good faith implementation of the governing constitutional principles").

110. *See* Welch 83–91.

111. *Ante*, at 27.

112. *Ante*, at 27–28.

113. *Cf. People Who Care* v. *Rockford Bd. of Ed. School Dist. No. 205*, 961 F. 2d 1335, 1338 (CA7 1992) (Easterbrook, J.) ("Would it be necessary to adjudicate the obvious before adopting (or permitting the parties to agree on) a remedy . . . ?").

114. *See ante*, at 18–20.

115. *See, e.g., Swann*, 402 U.S., at 24–25; *North Carolina Bd. of Ed.*, 402 U.S., at 46; *Montgomery County Bd. of Ed.*, 395 U.S., at 232.

116. *See* Orfield, Metropolitan School Desegregation: Impacts on Metropolitan Society, in Pursuit of a Dream Deferred: Linking Housing and Education Policy 121, 125.

117. *See* No Child Left Behind Act of 2001, Title V, Part C, 115 Stat. 1806, 20 U.S. C. §7231 *et seq.* (2000 ed., Supp. IV); 34 CFR §§280.2, 280.4 (2006) (implementing regulations).

118. *Ante*, at 8.

119. *See generally* N. Thompson & C. Marr, *Building for Learning: Seattle Public Schools Histories, 1862–2000* (2002).

120. *See supra*, at 12–14.

121. *See* Brief for Respondents in No. 05–908, p. 42.

122. *Ante*, at 4.

123. *See* App. in 05–915, p. 20.

124. *Id.*, at 21

125. *Ante*, at 6–7.

126. *Ante*, at 6; *ante*, at 15–16 (opinion of the Court).

127. Siqueland 116–117. *See also* Hanawalt 31; Pub. L. 95–561, Tit. VI (1978) (prescribing percentage enrollment requirements for "minority" students); Siqueland 55 (discussing Department of Health, Education, and Welfare's definition of "minority").

128. *Ante*, at 16.

129. *See supra*, at 46–48.

130. *See supra*, at 45.

131. *See ante*, at 13–15.

132. *Hampton II*, 102 F. Supp. 2d, at 370.

133. *See id.,* at 380 ("The very analysis for dissolving desegregation

decrees supports continued maintenance of a desegregated system as a compelling state interest").

134. 458 U.S. 457.

135. *Id.*, at 462–463, 483.

136. *Id.*, at 483–487.

137. 458 U.S., at 472, n. 15.

138. 458 U.S., at 472, n. 15.

139. *Id.*, at 473.

140. *Ibid.* (internal quotation marks and citation omitted).

141. *See supra*, at 12.

142. *Ibid.*

143. Welch 23 (footnotes omitted).

144. *See id.*, at 24–28.

145. *Id.*, at 25.

146. *Id.*, at 83–91.

147. *See* Education Commission of the States, Open Enrollment: 50-State Report (2007), online at http://mb2.ecs.org/reports/Report.aspx?id=268.

148. Ark. Code Ann. §6–18–206(f)(1), as amended 2007 Ark. Gen. Acts 552 (2007).

149. Ohio Rev. Code Ann. §3313.98(B)(2)(b)(iii) (Lexis Supp. 2006).

150. §3313.98 (F)(1)(a).

151. Conn. Gen. Stat. §10–266aa(b)(2) (2007).

152. §10–226a.

153. Conn. Agencies Regs. §10–226e-3(b) (1999).

154. §§10–226e-5(a) and (c)(4).

155. *See Sheff* v. *O'Neill*, 238 Conn. 1, 678 A. 2d 1267 (1996).

156. *Id.*, at 42, 678 A. 2d, at 1289.

157. *See supra*, at 27.

158. *Supra*, at 4.

159. *See* Appendix A, *infra*.

160. *See supra,* at 37–45.

161. *See supra,* at 20–21.

162. *See ante*, at 26–27 (Thomas, J., concurring); *Grutter*, 539 U.S., at 353–354 (Thomas, J., concurring in part and dissenting in part).

163. See *ante*, at 40–41 (plurality opinion); *see also ante*, at 26 (Thomas, J., concurring).

164. *Ante*, at 40–41. See also *Parents Involved VII*, 426 F. 3d, at 1222 (Bea, J., dissenting) ("The way to end racial discrimination is to stop discriminating by race").

165. See *Adarand Constructors, Inc.*, 515 U.S., at 237 ("[S]trict scrutiny" in this context is "[not] 'strict in theory, but fatal in fact'" (quoting *Fullilove*, 448 U.S., at 519 (Marshall, J., concurring in judgment))).

166. *Ante*, at 28.

167. See Part I, *supra*, at 2–21.

168. *Milliken*, 418 U.S., at 783 (Marshall, J., dissenting). *See also* C. Sumner, Equality Before the Law: Unconstitutionality of Separate Colored Schools in Massachusetts, in 2 The Works of Charles Sumner 327, 371 (1849) ("The law contemplates not only that all be taught, but that all shall be taught together"). *See* Part II, *supra*, at 21–37.

169. *Ante*, at 17–18 (opinion of Kennedy, J.).

170. See Parts III–IV, *supra*, at 37–57.

171. See Part V, *supra*, at 57–63.

172. See *ante*, at 39–41 (plurality opinion) (comparing Jim Crow segregation to Seattle and Louisville's integration polices); *ante*, at 28–32 (Thomas, J., concurring).

173. *Ante*, at 40 (plurality opinion).

174. *See ante*, at 39 (plurality opinion).

175. *Ante*, at 17 (Kennedy, J., concurring in part and concurring in judgment).

176. See *Cooper v. Aaron*, 358 U.S. 1 (1958).

INDEX

Adarand Constructors, Inc. v. Peña, 67–68

African Americans. *See* Blacks

Alito, Samuel, 30, 33

Arbery, Ahmaud, 6

attendance zones, 9, 52, 84

balancing. *See* diversity

Baltimore City College (City), 35

Baltimore City, segregation in, 6

Baltimore Polytechnic (Poly), 35

Baltimore School for the Arts (BSA), 35

Baltimore, minorities in, 35–36

Barrett, Amy Coney, 33

Blacks: children, 6, 8, 26, 42, 44, 74, 100; fall enrollment percentage, 102; imbalance, 47–48; leaving South, 9, 12; parents, 44; percentage of students in schools (1968–2011), 15; public school attendance, 1; SAT scores, 35–37; schools, 19, 44–46, 55, 92; students, 44–47, 52, 54, 75, 92

Board of Ed. of City School Dist. of New York v. Harris, 63, 66, 78

Bond, Julian, 16

Breyer, Stephen, 3, 5; challenging legal convention, 26–29; *Parents Involved in Community Schools* v. *Seattle School District No. 1* dissent, 39–105; power of dissent from, 30–34; principal dissent of, 19–25. See also *Parents Involved in Community Schools* v. *Seattle School District No. 1* (dissent)

Brown v. *Board of Education,* 2, 5, 8, 39, 99; aftermath of decision in, 51, 97; breaking promise of, 34–37; challenging legal convention, 26–29; dissent in, 13–14; focusing upon primary and secondary

Index

Brown v. *Board of Education (cont.)*
schools, 76; hope and promise of, 100–101; path set by, 98; power of dissent concerning, 30–34; pre-*Brown* state laws, 43; segregation at time of, 96

Burger, Warren, 27, 61

Bush, George W., 16, 18

busing, 9, 22, 41, 43, 58, 71, 81–84, 89, 96; court-imposed guidelines and, 52–54; Seattle Plan and, 47–49

Bustop, Inc. v. *Los Angeles Bd. of Ed.*, 2

California, segregation in, 6

Casazza, Jaren, 3

Civil Rights Act (1964), 7

Civil Rights Commission Study, 91–92

Connecticut Supreme Court, 93–94

Cooper v. *Aaron*, 9, 31

de facto segregation, 24, 26, 29, 43, 63–64, 77–78, 94

de jure segregation, 26, 43, 59, 63, 65–66, 77, 111n15

desegregation, 8–9, 31, 41, 52, 62; decree, 12, 17, 100; dissent in context of, 30–34; efforts, 23, 47, 77, 84; order, 14, 16, 53, 56–57, 88, 119n99; plans, 12, 22–24, 40, 43, 52, 76, 82, 88–89, 91–93; policies, 82

direct precedent, 88–90

dissent, power of, 30–34. *See also Parents Involved in Community Schools* v. *Seattle School District No. 1* (dissent)

diversity, 18, 22, 73, 77, 85, 86, 95, 97

Driver, Justin, 3

Eisenhower, Dwight, 8

Emergency School Aid Act, 86

Equal Protection Clause, 61, 63, 65, 69–70, 86, 88–89, 95, 96

Faubus, Orval, 8

federal courts, 14, 17, 27, 32, 41, 63–64, 89

Flint, Tacy, 3

Floyd, George, 6

Fourteenth Amendment, 28–29, 65, 86

Francis M. Wood High School, 35

Frederick Douglass High School, 35–36

Ginsburg, Ruth Bader, 33

Gorsuch, Neil, 33

Greenhouse, Linda, 3

Grutter v. *Bollinger*, 67–69, 72, 76–77, 80, 87, 97–98

Illinois, segregation in, 6

Index

Jackson, Andrew, 31
Johnson v. *California,* 67–68

Kagan, Elena, 33
Kavanaugh, Brett, 33
Kennedy, Anthony, 19, 33

Latinos, 42; New Jersey students, 6–7; public school attendance, 1
legal convention, challenging, 26–29
legal standard, 61–73; compelling interest, 73–79; narrow tailoring, 79–87. *See also Parents Involved in Community Schools* v. *Seattle School District No. 1* (dissent)
Little Rock, Arkansas, insurrection in, 8–9
Louisville, Kentucky, segregation case of, 17–25; challenging legal convention, 26–29; court-imposed guidelines, 52–54; current lawsuit, 57; current plan, 55–57; before lawsuit, 51–52; *Parents* dissent, 51–57; Project Renaissance, 54–55

magnet schools, 55–57, 71, 84
mandatory pupil reassignment, 93
Marshall, Thurgood, 13–14
Maryland, segregation in, 6
McLaurin v. *Oklahoma State Regents for Higher Ed.,* 76

Milliken v. *Bradley,* 5, 12–14
Milliken, William, 12
minorities, 70, 86, 97; minority group isolation, 83; percentage in schools by race, 105; populations, 47, 50

narrow tailoring, 79–85
National Association for the Advancement of Colored People (NAACP), 62; first legal challenge, 45–47; second legal challenge, 47
New York, segregation in, 6
Nixon, Richard, 32
Norfolk, Virginia, resegregated schools in, 74–75
North Carolina Bd. of Ed. v. *Swann,* 61–62

O'Connor, Sandra Day, 33

Parent Assistance Centers, 56
Parents Involved in Community Schools v. *Seattle School District No. 1* (dissent), 2, 39–40; applying legal standard, 73–87; conclusions, 96–101; consequences, 90–95; direct precedent, 88–90; facts, 40–61; history, 57–61; legal standard, 61–73; Louisville, 51–57; Seattle, 44–51
Powell, Lewis, 27–28

Index

Regents of the University of California v. *Bakke,* 28, 67, 89

Rehnquist, William, 33

resegregation, 14, 16–17, 19, 21, 23, 36, 40, 43; de facto resegregation, 74, 94; trends in, 102–5

Resegregation Cases, 2–3, 5, 17–25; breaking promise of *Brown,* 34–37; challenging legal convention, 26–29; power of dissent in, 30–34

Roberts, John, 33; Seattle and Louisville cases, 17–19

SAT scores, 35–37

Scalia, Antonin, 33; Seattle and Louisville cases, 17–19

school board policies and actions, 43

schools: nonwhite public schools, 7; resegregation of, 14–16; stagnating integration of, 6–17; unitary status, 16

scrutiny review, 68

Seattle Plan, 89–90; current plan, 50–51; implementing, 47–49; NAACP legal challenges, 45–47; preliminary challenges to, 44–45; segregation prior to, 45; student choice, 49–50

Seattle, Washington, segregation case of, 17–25; challenging legal convention, 26–29; *Parents* dissent, 44–51. *See also* Seattle Plan

segregation, 1–2; Little Rock, Arkansas, insurrection, 8–9; most segregated states, 6; in primary and secondary schools, 76–77; public school suffering from, 6–17; Seattle and Louisville cases, 17–25. *See also de facto* segregation; *de jure* segregation; desegregation

Shackelford, Stephen, 3

Sotomayor, Sonia, 33

Souter, David, 33

Stevens, John Paul, 33; dissent of, 19–20

strategic site selection, 84

strict scrutiny, 21, 67–69, 71–73, 87

student choice, 22, 43, 54, 58, 71, 79, 81, 93, 96. *See also* Blacks; Latinos; whites

Swann v. *Charlotte-Mecklenburg Bd. of Ed.,* 20–21, 27–28, 70, 76, 78, 89, 96–99; challenging legal convention, 26–29

Sweatt v. *Painter,* 76

Thomas, Clarence, 18–19, 33, 59, 66, 72, 78–79, 95, 99

U.S. Commission on Civil Rights, 82

U.S. Constitution, 28–29, 39–40. *See also* Fourteenth Amendment

Index

U.S. Supreme Court, 2; counter-
acting moral leadership of,
9–10; decision intervals, 7–8;
Milliken v. *Bradley,* 12–14;
power of dissent in, 30–34;
suburban white flight, 17;
Resegregation Cases, 17–25
United States, segregation in
schools of, 6–17

Washington v. *Seattle School
Dist. No. 1,* 89–90, 99
Western High School, 35

whites: nonwhite public schools,
7; percentage in schools
attended by Black students,
103–4; percentage of
students in schools (1968–
2011), 15; public school
attendance, 1. *See also* Blacks;
Latinos
Worchester v. *Georgia,* 31

Zaslawsky v. *Bd. of Ed. of Los
Angeles City Unified School
Dist.,* 64–65